Veli Ndabas
Prayer

Let Me Be The One!
Lord my Heavenly Father, let me be the one that helps people choose to live fully today. Let me be the message of hope today and beyond.

Let me be the sign of hope today. Let me be the window of hope. Let me bring hope so that everyone who sees me, hears me, reads me and thinks of me changes to the better.

May nobody have evil thoughts about me and if they do, please change their hearts and minds. Please give me the strength and courage to overcome the challenges I'll face today, let me never doubt myself.

Let me have a bigger vision of myself and always be reminded that I was created by you, the Master Creator, to live a beautiful and influential life for Your glory and for the good of others, Amen!

Set Your Soul
On Fire!

Set Your Soul On Fire

Setting your soul on fire is about:

1. Searching for yourself and observing your natural inclinations and passions.
2. Finding a long lost you and claiming it back.
3. Winning the real long lost you back from the world of confusion and away from unhealthy thoughts and beliefs, unhealthy habits, toxic relationships, unhealthy lifestyle and activities not aligned to your dreams.
4. Working on the real you to unleash your personal greatness.

Life is all about self-discovery, don't be a follower that swallows everything you receive, be a great student of life that questions, analyses and interrogates the things you receive, see and hear.

SPEAKER | CONSULTANT | LIFE COACH | AUTHOR

WHAT I DO

As an experienced Motivational Speaker, Business Coach and Consultant, I'm focussed on delivering the tools, insight and expertise your organisation needs to become more competitive, productive and motivated for success.

I help people align their beliefs, thoughts, habits and goals and live meaningful and purposeful lives.

WHO I WORK WITH

I currently offer my services to clients that include

- Businesses
- Corporates
- Seminars
- Conferences
- Any groups

I have successfully partnered with a wide range of corporate clients as diverse as Ford Motor Company SA, Standard Bank, Barloworld Equipment, Emerald Resorts and Casinos, SC Johnson, Altech Netstar, Builders Warehouse, UNISA, University of Johannesburg, Colgate Palmolive, Rand Water, amongst many others.

My services include:

- Corporate and motivational speaking: Popular topics include: You Have The Power To Live Your Dreams, Be Engineered To WIN & Live In The Moment.
- Business consulting: Helping teams work seamlessly, strategically and productively, optimising team effectiveness and efficiency, implementing powerful review processes and tools to improve clarity and direction.

- Corporate coaching: Individual coaching for business leaders to help maximise effectiveness, influence others and motivate teams for success. Targeted coaching to transcend to a higher level of achievement.
- Skills coaching: Time management, delegation skills, leadership skills, emotional intelligence skills, and team management.

As a published author, I also offer three books on personal development, motivation, inspiration and empowerment – available at https://www.velindaba.com/store-2/

WHAT MAKES ME DIFFERENT

I have a healthy mix of passion and insight into professional and personal development, and I'm driven to help companies produce meaningful results in this area. I work with businesses that know they can achieve more but don't know how to get there, that are busy but not getting the results they are looking for. I help them to create high-performance teams and leaders that are self-aware, engaged and purposeful. My fusion of real-life stories and conversational techniques in my work connect with my clients and audiences at an intimate, intense and individual level.

Previous Experience

As a Mechanical Engineer with a BSC in Management Science, Diploma in Mechanical Engineering, and Project management, I have over 12 years working in blue chip organizations. I worked as a junior engineer up to senior engineering manager and I was responsible for staff recruitment and development- mentoring and coaching, project management, budget planning and control, strategy formulation to implementation and more.

Delighted clients:

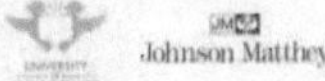
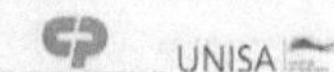

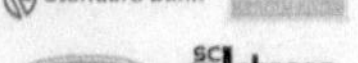

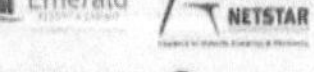
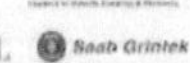

Cell: 083 304 9773 • **Email:** veli@velindaba.com
Web: www.velindaba.com

Telephone: +27 10 591 1197 • **Skype:** velindaba
Twitter: @VeliNdaba

LinkedIn: www.linkedin.com/in/Velindaba
Youtube: www.youtube.com/user/Velindaba

For booking call or email: veli@velindaba.com • 083 304 9773

CONTENTS

1. Introduction

"You cannot dream yourself into a character; you must hammer and forge yourself one."
— *Henry David Thoreau*

We spend a ton of time investing in things that numb us to the reality of how short life is — things like scrolling the internet for hours on end or watching TV to the point of restlessness. Entertainment is fun, but how much time do we save for ourselves? How often do we set aside dedicated time for personal development, where we are learning and growing in a way that defines our existence? Always remember that your income seldom exceeds your personal development. How would you like me to help you get ahead in your journey towards your dreams?

A "Drama Mamma" is a man or woman who has caught the virus of victimitis excusitis. All that such people do is complain about how bad things are for them instead of applying their God-given power to make things better. They take instead of giving, criticise instead of creating and worry instead of working.

Let today and beyond be the day you build strength to fight any average from getting anywhere near you. Never be a "Drama Mamma".

"It's the honest truth that some people's dreams are tied to yours. If you therefore don't achieve your dreams, not only your life will suffer but many other people's dreams will never see the light of day."— Veli Ndaba - 'The Engineered Mind - to WIN.'

So, resolve today to own your stuff and be the best of whatever you are. May the rest of your life be the best of your life!

Is it fundamentally sound? Most people never divorce their initial ideas that don't prove to be fundamentally sound simply because they'll lose face and they'll have to admit that they made a mistake by doing it. Sadly, most people stay on the fundamentally unsound situations and paths forever because they don't want to admit they made a mistake. Fundamentally, if something is wrong, it should be stopped immediately, even if you've put in your everything and spent lots of time in it.

The sooner you cut your losses, the quicker you get onto the right path — that's fundamentally sound. We tend to stay married to ideas, habits and situations that no longer serve us well. It shows strength and wisdom to admit that if it's wrong, it's wrong and don't feel embarrassed about it, it's your life after all.

A person who makes a mistake and does not correct it, is making another mistake, period!

If you don't change your ways, you'll stay in the same situation and blame it on everything else but you.
You have the key to change your life by continually asking yourself this important question, 'Is what I'm doing fundamentally sound? Is it in line with my goals and dreams?'
I love Whitney Houston's song: One Moment In Time! She says, "Each day I live. I want to be a day to give the best of me. I'm only one, but not alone.
My finest day is yet unknown. I want one moment in time when I'm more than I thought I could be. When all of my dreams are a heartbeat away and the answers are all up to me. I've lived to be the very best, I want it all, No time for less. I've laid the plans, Now lay the chance here in my hands."

2. The Power Of Purpose

"There are two questions that we have to ask ourselves. The 1st is, "Where am I going?" and the 2nd is, "Who will go with me?" If you ever get these questions in the wrong order, you are in trouble." — Dr Howard Thurman

Purpose gives your life a meaning. It helps you focus on what matters most and ignore distractions.

If you don't have a clear purpose, it's so easy to be taken advantage of and side-tracked by things that don't add any value in your life. When you have a clear purpose, you value your time more, ignore time-wasters, take full responsibility for your life, accept hardships of life and are driven by the excitement of the person you are becoming, not just of accumulating things. Purpose, to me, is a path that one has to take in order to reach their destiny.

Imagine you are in city A and there are so many cities you can connect to — B to Z.

Now, which city you connect to should be chosen based on your passion and strengths. That's why when you ask most people what their purpose is, they say "To help people!" Whether it's the homeless, elderly, etc., but it's helping people.

The main question is, "How will you accomplish that purpose of helping people?" The lowest form of helping people is to reach out for donations.
This is being dependent on others to help you help others.
The highest form of living your purpose is using your own gifts and talents to raise money in order to fulfil your purpose — work gives dignity. The way you find your gifts and talents is by studying yourself, observing your passions and strengths — those things you like and do so well. Socrates, one of the greatest philosophers said, "Know thyself." That's what he meant. Studying yourself is a long- term process. A normal university degree takes about three to four years of serious studying — tests, assignments, research and examinations. However difficult and challenging the process, you have to stick it out. This, I've found to be the same with finding your gifts and talents, it's a process that's full of challenges. All of us have these hidden treasures within us, saying you don't know what they are won't help you, you have to study yourself.

In simple terms, your gifts and talents are your vehicle to accomplish your purpose. Remember, your purpose is just a path to connect you from where you are to where you desire to be and the means or vehicle to get there is your gifts and talents.

So, choose where you are going first and then choose the vehicle and partners that will help you get there.

3. How to build self-confidence

"Each time we face our fear, we gain strength, courage, and confidence in the doing." —Theodore Roosevelt

Self-confidence is the most attractive quality a person can have. Just think about it, how can anyone see how great you are if you can't see it yourself? Don't live down to expectations, go out there and do something remarkable!

As a professional speaker, life and business coach, author, entrepreneur, newspaper columnist and blogger, I'm often asked how I became this confident. I think I should share these important steps that will help you build your confidence.

Step 1: Think about what you can invest your time and energy into.

Thinking is a process where you generate different ideas. To think better, you need to ask better questions. Questions like:

- What can I do to improve my current situation?

- Write down different ideas that come to mind without qualifying them.

- How can this idea help me improve my situation? Be specific

- What skills do I need to make it happen? Write them down

- You need to be in a quiet place that will allow you to think and write your answers down on your 'Thinking Note Book' where you capture all your important ideas.

Step 2: Decide from the list of generated ideas above and choose one.

Decision-making is very critical. Whatever option you choose, stick to it until the end. The mantra/affirmation I use especially when I start a new project/goal is, "Whatever I start, I finish!" I say these words repeatedly, especially when doubt creeps in.

Step 3: Put a plan together.

A plan will help you get structured: It answers questions like:

- What you will do.

- How you will do it.

- Why you'll do it.

- When you will do it — with start and finish dates.

- What resources you'll need to accomplish this goal.

Step 4: Start - Massive Action.

We all have fears and doubts and the only way to deal with them is by having a proper plan in place and taking massive action. Starting is magical.

Step 5: Progress.

Progressing is a sure sign that you're moving forward, however little.

This injects you with energy and confidence. The more you see small amounts of progress, the more confident you become, it's a sign that you are in control. Now, this confidence and energy will surely keep you going and increase the pace and intensity.

Step 6: Achieving/Completion.

This is the final step in the process. The most important part of success is the person you become along the journey, not just rushing to completion and miss out on some important insights and beautiful views along the way.

This is how you build confidence. Confidence comes when you know you have a plan, process and a system to follow and taking massive action towards your goal. I wish you well!

4. Understand the law of harvest

"Those who work their land will have abundant food, but those who chase fantasies have no sense." — Proverbs 12v11

Life follows natural laws that are in place. Working against any of them, can only bring misery and pain. To me, it makes perfect sense to take some time to study and understand them. The law of the harvest states that you have to:

- plough the ground;

- plant the seed;

- water the seed;

- reap the harvest.

The above steps look simple to me. They are not easy, but they are simple. Simple because they are not complicated to follow, the sequence is clear. Implementing them requires discipline, focus and patience which is not easy.

Remember, there are two kinds of pain in the world, the pain of discipline and that of regret. The pain of discipline happens in the moment when you do what you have to do, as difficult and painful as it is. The pain of regret weighs heavily at the end, when you avoided the pain of discipline. These are "could have been's; should have been's; wish I had known better, etc." When this happens, that's when you know you messed up.

Don't envy the harvest of the rich. Envy their planting. So, when it is time to sow, sow and when it is time to harvest, you will harvest. Obey this rule for your own good.

Every day, you have the right and wrong seeds with you. One thing for sure, if you plant the wrong ones, they won't come out positive. Plant the right seeds and water them through repetition and continue with it even though it looks like nothing is happening. In the right time, the good plant will come out. When the good things that you have planted — by following the law of the harvest — come out, you'll hear people saying, "you are a genius; you have green fingers; you are lucky; you are a magician; etc." It's all about obeying the simple law of harvest.

Here's something important you also need to know about this law: while there may be many things in life you wish to harvest, not every seed you plant will grow, just accept that, it's part of the equation.

Finally, like a farmer, keep expecting and believing that your due season is coming. Declare that the good you have planted in your life will manifest. Every season has an end for a harvest to begin. Embrace the process!

5. I'll do it until...

"Far better it is to dare mighty things, to win glorious triumphs, even though checkered by failure, than to take rank with those poor spirits who neither enjoy much nor suffer much, because they live in the gray twilight that knows neither victory nor defeat."
— Theodore Roosevelt

People of substance who have achieved great success have this common attitude and philosophy about them that says, "I will do it until..." Here, I'm talking about success as an inner ideal which is persistently followed with courage. This means defining a goal and having the resolve to complete it, no matter what.

It's all about saying, I'll do it or die. It's about promising yourself that you'll read the necessary books until your skills change. That you'll go to the seminars until you get the hang of it. That you'll do it until it makes sense. That you'll practice it until you get it right.

That you won't give up until you get where you want to be, however hard or long that is, step by step, piece by piece, book by book, semi- nar by seminar, doing it until…

'Until' is a very important word here, it's key. It means you'll never give up. It means you'll never miss the chance to pay the price until you learn and grow. It's only when you grow that you discover some of life's great treasures, only when you are prepared to pay the price.
It's this attitude that sets high achievers apart. They become fruitful and productive. To be fruitful and productive means to be able to produce far more than you need for yourself so that you can bless others as well.
It is this winners' attitude that I, Veli Ndaba, decided to adopt hence you are reading this article — I Will Do It Until… I'm challenging you as well to adopt it and let's join hands in making this beautiful world of ours a much better place than we found it.

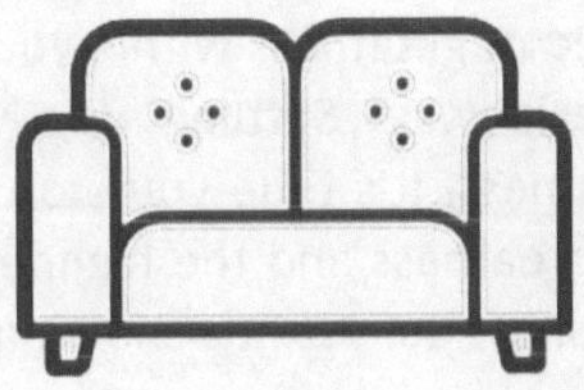

6. Refuse to settle

"The unexamined life is not worth living." — Socrates

If you had your life to live all over again, without a doubt, you would achieve much more than you have achieved thus far. You have so much potential within you than you can ever begin to imagine. What you have achieved thus far, is only a tip of the iceberg of what is possible for you. Appreciate and be happy with what you have and what you are, but don't settle. The excitement of life comes from the expectation of something new and different. Predictability kills excitement and cre- ativity. Nelson Mandela said, "There is no passion to be found playing small — in settling for a life that is less than the one you are capable of living."

When you settle, you kill the spark and you miss out on what you could've been. He further said, "Af- ter climbing a great hill, one only finds that there are many more hills to climb." So, when you achieve some goal you set for yourself, you realise that there's more out there then you initially thought. If you never try, you'll never know what you are capable of.

Why wait for great people to come and change the world if you have a seed of greatness within you to do the same in your own special way. 'Settling' deprives you and the world from greatness. It's time you stop being a fugitive from your own greatness and the highness that is within you. It's time to show up, yes, it's show time.

Don't cheat the world of your contribution, give it what you've got! Let's do this!

7. Are you a victim of wrong priorities?

"It's not enough to be busy... The question is: What are we busy about?"— Henry David Thoreau

I once came across these following words which got me really thinking, "My biggest regrets in life are being too damn nice, apologising when I didn't do anything wrong, and making unworthy people a priority in my life."

The undeniable truth is that you always have time for the things you put first in your life. This without a doubt will be reflected in the results you produce. Your priorities are definitely not what you say they are, but they are revealed by what you do. As a speaker and life coach, I get to share this with my audiences as it is fundamentally important.

That's why self-awareness is so important. Self-awareness leads you to a place deep down within you that knows that in order to create magic in the world, you firstly have to own the magic within yourself.

It helps you differentiate between your beliefs that are merely cultural constraints and those that are truths. It helps you also differentiate between the trustworthy voice of your intuition and the persuasive pronouncements of your fears. True freedom is never received, but rather released from within.

Self-awareness helps you know better, choose better and align with the highest that's within you. It also makes you open-minded. The truth is that open-minded people don't care to be right, they care to understand. They don't fix the blame, they fix the problem. They know that everything is about understanding.

What you put first or prioritise, gives most results in your life. So, if you don't like your current results, it's not because the conditions are unfavourable for you, it's because of what you have put first in your list of priorities. It's priorities that make winners as well as losers. Yes, let me say it again, winners win because of their habits, not because they are good people. Same with those that lose, they lose because of their habits, not because they are bad people, NO!

What you put first in your life, makes you, it's as simple as that. If you are not getting the results you want, I suggest that you seriously review your priorities. What does your 24-hour day look like? The best way to do it, is to write down everything you've done each day for the past week. That will show you what you put first in your life and then start to correct what needs to be corrected.

What you have achieved thus far is only a tip of the iceberg compared to what you are capable of achieving, always remember that.

8. Fail fast

"Failure is simply the opportunity to begin again, this time more intelligently." — Henry Ford

Most regrets in life come from the failure of not failing at all, or failing too late. You see, failing too late doesn't help at all. This is because of waiting for your ducks to all get in a row which more often than not doesn't happen.

Success has never been a great teacher, it is failure that is and has always been a great teacher. So, the faster you fail, the quicker you learn to correct your approach, mistakes and your errors in judgement. Obviously, I don't mean that you must just blindly fail, do your homework, but be very mindful of the window of opportunity. We wait and wait for the right time and the right people to come along until time runs out of time. When we realise that we waited too long hoping for the best, we then panic, make mistakes and never recover.

You are like a ship in a harbour; it's safe there but that's not what ships are built for. You are meant to be out there on the sea and be the best of whatever you are. The truth never ceases to exist because it is ignored; it remains the truth until it is recognised.

Theodore Roosevelt said it so well, "Far better is it to dare mighty things, to win glorious triumphs, even though checkered by failure... than to rank with those poor spirits who neither enjoy nor suffer much, because they live in a gray twilight that knows not victory nor defeat." These powerful words always fuel my fire.

Failing fast helps you correct what needs to be corrected while you still have time to do so. Failing fast reveals your true friends that are worth keeping; it helps you re-calibrate your compass and most importantly, it helps you rectify your errors in judgment about life itself.

Fail fast, that's what life is all about. Let's give it a go!

9. Create the best version of yourself

I Deserve This... I Deserve That... "To get what you want, you have to deserve what you want." — Charlie Munger

The quickest way to accelerate your growth in whatever you do, is to get rid of the mentality that the world owes you something - that's self-entitlement. This seems to be a disease most people suffer from.

The world is not yet a crazy enough place to reward a whole bunch of undeserving people, it is that simple. Whatever you feel you deserve, claim it through your work, not words.

You have potential to live a great life, but that potential will remain just that until you convert it through deliberate and intelligent work.

10. What is stealing your greatness?

"Pride is the parent of destruction; pride eats the mind and the heart and the soul alive." — Anne Rice

We often wonder why we are not where we are supposed to be in life. Well, the answer lies in us. Here are the three main thieves of greatness:

1. **Too much pride** — A person with too much pride always looks down on people and things and of course, as long as you are looking down, you can't see something that is above you - that is meant to lift you up. Too much pride is concerned with who is right rather than what is right. A person with too much pride will never take any advice; will never say please help me and will never say thank you nor I'm sorry, I was wrong!

2. **Stubbornness** — Stubborn people may appear to be sweet and understanding to your advice.

They will take the advice and thank you for it and feel so sorry that they missed out on this important information in their lives, but won't implement it because they are not willing to adjust irrespective of how important the advice is. They are set in their ways! They'll always justify by using 'BUT...'

3. **Being overly sensitive** — This is about taking everything personal. With this person, you must always be nice and a bit slow when you talk with them.

   You must, for most of the time, tip-toe around issues because if you are straight with them, they get upset and even cry. The best way to wake someone up quickly is to raise your voice at them a bit. Some will hate you for raising your voice whereas the majority will thank you for waking them up.

The truth is, we all get caught up by these thieves from time to time and self-awareness will help you guard against them. Just take stock of the past week and see how your greatness has been stolen by these three thieves and you'll be so amazed.

11. It's all in your attitude

"The pessimist complains about the wind; the optimist expects it to change; the realist adjusts the sails."
— William Arthur Ward

We have been socialised to believe that good things come to those who wait. This, unfortunately, was literally taken as gospel truth without qualifying its applicability. To me, growing up means questioning things that you hear around you instead of just accepting them as they are.
Jim Rohn said, "It's not the economy that will determine your next five years, it's your philosophy."

So, if there are errors in your philosophy or judgement, then, you'll miss the boat to success because you'll prioritise all the wrong things in your life.

Your philosophy is your attitude towards life. If your attitude is that the world owes you something, you'll be unreasonable, miserable and bitter until you change it, or else death takes you. If, however, your philosophy is that: "if it's to be, it's all up to me!"

Then, success and greatness will be yours until the end of time. Your fire to get things done lies purely in your attitude, it's that simple.

The truth is, each day is a special day because it's never been experienced before and will never be experienced ever again in future.
Today is like you; you are special and unique because this world has never experienced anything like you. You have unique gifts and talents, and failure to express them, makes you ordinary and frustrated because you are not operating from the place of power and truth.
Opportunities are truly like sunrises in our lives, missing the early morning means missing the sunrise. Your philosophy or attitude is more like a compass, if wrongly set, you miss your destination. The good news, however, is that it can be re-calibrated. For me, Veli Ndaba, coaching and mentoring worked like a charm. It helped me re-calibrate my compass and hence you are reading this article.

So, are you just sitting there and complaining about the wind? Or are you waiting and expecting it to change? Or are you taking advantage of the wind in your life? Well, the choice is all yours, it's all in your attitude. The world has long been waiting for your stuff, take it out!

12. Faith is the beginning of wisdom

"Faith is taking the first step even when you don't see the whole staircase."
— Martin Luther King, Jr

Yes, faith is believing when it is beyond the power of reason to believe. It is in the darkness that you can clearly see the stars. Faith is knowing that even though you have nothing now, better things are coming.

Faith allows you to suffer with meaning. Suffering with meaning is about taking the pain of life's beatings, disappointments, hurts, delays (which are often called failures) and rejections in your stride and say, "Better days are coming and I'll hold on in spite of" Life has shown again and again that faith is seeing the invisible, believing the unbelievable and that surely leads to one receiving the impossible. You see, we all get stuck in certain situations from time to time, but what gets you out of it is focusing your mind beyond it. That is the reason we are told to walk by faith not by sight.

I've, in so many instances, been so taken aback by the power of faith where I had trusted without reservation and I finally got what initially seemed impossible.

Yes, you may be going through a lot right now, but always know that better days are coming. Your faith is surely stretched when nothing works and your life seems to be falling apart. Always remember that doubt creates mountains, whereas faith moves them.
When you have faith in yourself, you don't have to rely on others to believe in you. So, accept what it is, let go of what was and have faith in what will be. The world has long been waiting for your greatness and now is your time to unleash it and shine brighter!

13. It is what it is, embrace it!

"I know God will not give me anything I can't handle. I just wish that he didn't trust me so much."
— Mother Teresa

I've visited different places and read different books trying to understand why certain people go through unbearably difficult situations and conditions, risking their lives in the process of trying to achieve something. To me, handling something has a very deep meaning. It's like a movement of some sort, if its leader or founder dies, those that believe in the idea continue with it until its fulfilment. Something keeps them grounded, however challenging the conditions.

What I've found to be constantly keeping me grounded whenever the storms of life angrily blow at me, is the final picture on the other side of the angry storm. The only way, I've found through research as well as trial and error, of developing a close relationship with this future picture, that is much better than the current one, is constantly keeping that future picture in front of me as much as I possibly can.

This picture eventually forms in the subconscious mind and this process is called visualisation. It's undeniably true that whatever you focus on the longest, becomes your strongest.

Pursuing your dreams is a very hard and lonely road to travel. It's lonely not because there's no one around you, but because no one truly understands your reasons and willingness to pay the heavy, and at times, the ultimate price just to achieve that future picture.
Benjamin Disraeli said, "I've brought myself, by long meditation, to the conviction that a human being with a settled purpose must accomplish it. And that nothing can resist a will which will stake even existence upon its fulfilment." These words challenged my thinking, and even more, Steve Biko's words, "It's better to die for an idea that will live than to live for an idea that will die." These words inspire me to face my angry storms because I know that what is possible for one, is possible for others too.

I've visited Robben Island where Nelson Mandela and many others were imprisoned just to get the sense of what they went through. I've also recently visited the Auschwitz Camps in Poland to get a sense of what Dr Victor Frankl and many others went through.

Yes, I've had a fair share of challenges in my life but nothing near what these people went through.
The only thing that made these individuals endure these horrible conditions was the vision of the future beyond the suffering.

So, if you want a better future, be willing to go through the angry storms, embrace that because it is what it is. I was born to re-ignite your fire.

14. Are you a river or a dam?

"We make a living by what we get. We make a life by what we give." — Winston S. Churchill

They both receive water from the rain, but one is thriving with life while the other is toxic. The rainwater the river receives, it shares and conveys it downstream hence it stays fresh. The dam however, always feels entitled to receive and keep. Because it doesn't share, whatever it receives and keep becomes salty and toxic. Thank you and gratitude are not part of the dam's vocabulary. It always feels entitled to receive but not obligated to share.

When you have adopted a river's mentality, you are free, you are fresh and you thrive with life. You don't waste your time worrying so much about the future happenings, your faith keeps you going. You don't get possessed by your possessions.

When you have adopted the dam's mindset, you are driven by entitlement. You always want to receive and keep to show the world how much you've got.

Unfortunately, what you keep becomes stale and toxic as it is not meant to be kept but shared. A person with this mindset is never happy and grateful about anything hence saying thank you and I'm sorry don't exist in their vocabulary, because they think everything is about them. This is a sad way to live.

I'm often asked where do I get all the time, energy and these ideas I write about, most people don't get it.
I always have them flowing through me, hence I share them any time and any day. Some ask me why I don't wait until I put them in a book? I think this is a difference between me and many others, I was born to inspire and empower people to save themselves from self-sabotage and therefore waiting until I write a book will not achieve this.

I have written and published three books and for me, I am happy. My belief is that we are blessed to bless others. Winston Churchill said, "We make a living by what we receive and make a life by what we give."

Appreciate life and be grateful for your blessings, however small they may seem.

15. What is stopping you?

"There is no passion to be found in settling for a life that is less than the one you are capable of living."
— Nelson Mandela

When I give my talks, I sometimes share a story about a woman who climbed and reached the top of Mt Everest, the highest mountain in the world. When asked how she felt that she had conquered the highest mountain in the world, she answered by saying: "I never conquered the mountain and no one will ever conquer the mountain, I only conquered the fears and limitations in me." Wow, this was seriously profound.

When you really conquer the negative thoughts, ideas and wrong advice that create False Expectations Appearing Real (FEAR), you'll live your life freely and your life will be used as a good example for generations to come. So, what is really stopping you from doing the thing/s that you so want to do?

I truly believe that it's much better and rewarding to look back on your life and say: "Wow, I can't believe I did that." Than to look back on your life with tears in your eyes saying: "Oh, how I wish I did that." This will haunt you for the rest of your life.

For me, low self-esteem and underestimating my capabilities and potential stopped me as they created FEAR in me.

I couldn't see myself achieving any of my goals, I was under the impression that the answers were lying outside of me. I just woke up one day in May 2011, and decided I didn't want to feel like that ever again, so I changed just like that. I have since learned that what you see in life entirely depends on what you are looking for.

I made a list of things I was scared of or feared, from small to big ones. I started off by confronting the small ones to gain confidence. I remember taking my boys to Gold Reef City for the rides. I told them I was going to confront my FEARS from that day on and I was going to ride all the roller-coasters that I was scared of.

They laughed at me and said, "Really?" I started riding on the Anaconda, Runaway train, Golden loop, etc. I rode them again and again, by the end of the day I was different. I realised that for all the years it was never about those roller-coasters but me, I allowed FEAR of NOTHING to steal my happiness and freedom. That's how I built my confidence and moved on to bigger things.

So, my advice to you:
1. First identify and write down the thing/s you fear;
2. Take one step forward to approach it;

3. Take the second step. Don't rush yourself, but do push yourself. Once you find yourself able to handle the first rung on your FEAR ladder with less anxiety,
4. Move to the next one. Once you begin to get comfortable with facing YOUR FEARS,
5. Don't stop.
6. Keep going!
The last thing is to get yourself a coach and/or mentor who will keep you focused and stay the course. You are God's highest form of creation, your gifts and talents were given to you to make this world a better place than you found it, flatly refuse to take them to your grave with you!

16. Are you doing what you should be doing?

"Do what is right, not what is easy nor what is popular."
— Roy T. Bennet

Doing the right thing gives you the feeling of peace and serenity, and you find yourself doing it again and again.

We've always been told that when you do what you love, you'll never work a single day in your life. Sometimes what you love is not the right thing for you to do in order to advance further in your life. This brings me to a concept of opportunity cost.

Most smart people understand the concept of opportunity cost, they just get it. The problem is that very few of them implement it. Let's say you are reading a 500 page book, you are now 350 pages in and you realise that it's not worth your while. However, there might be some valuable nuggets in the last 150 pages and it means you need to read for another three hours.

Now, the opportunity cost is not those three hours of reading the remaining pages, it's what else could you be reading. There are many great books out there, so you need to wisen up a little bit on how you choose them.

The worst thing you can do is to choose a bad book and miss out on great insightful books that may change your life forever.

In all areas of your life, learn to apply this opportunity cost concept by continually asking yourself these questions, "What else could I be doing instead of this?"; "Where else could I be instead of here?"; "What career could I be in?"; "Who else could I be learning from?"

I once read an article which indicated that the three biggest regrets of people are: 1. Who they chose as life partners, 2. The career they chose and 3.The education they had. And, to the extent, you regret only one of them, you'll be happier than people who regret two of them and so on. This made me put on my thinking cap and seriously evaluate my use of time, energy and money.

I can only hope that this awakens you. To be "awakened," you have to understand your life story and which events shaped you into the person you are today. Gaining clarity on these will help you learn more about your- self and why you behave in a certain way. This will increase your self-awareness level and help you gain clarity on what direction in life you should take. You are unique and special and that's what the world needs from you!

17. What sets your soul on fire?

"There are three things that a child can teach an adult: to be happy for no reason; to be always busy doing something; and to know how to demand, with all one's might, what one wants." — Paulo Coelho

It's crucial to find what sets your soul on fire and let it burn you to the ground. This is something that gives your life a meaning. All of us have some motivation of some sort. I define motivation as the desire to achieve that which you believe to be worthwhile.

Many people go through life never getting in touch with their greatness because of the lack of motivation to push themselves or because they have not found something that they believe to be worthwhile to challenge them. There's a poem by Thomas Gray that goes, "Full many a flower is born to blush unseen, and waste its sweetness on the desert air." True living is about expressing your greatness. It's when your soul is on fire and is being burned down to the ground.

Many people seem to go through life without displaying their talents and gifts. Writing these inspirational and empowering articles sets my soul on fire, I'm really burning to the ground right now and how I wish you could be seeing a broad smile on my face! It's something I am always looking forward to, it's my craft, not my job.

I am all about self-awareness as it helps you discover yourself. Now, here's how you can measure your motivation:
 How do you rate yourself in a scale of 1 — 5 in these following areas:

1. Mental attitude about yourself — Is it by Design or Default? - What do you believe is true for you?
2. Physical appearance and health? Do you really take good care of yourself? We cannot help getting older, but we don't have to get old. Many people get old before the time because they don't take good care of themselves.
3. Environment you find yourself in - is it desirable, is it conducive for your growth? Is it what you want it to be or you are just coasting along?
4. The job or career that you are involved in? Is it fulfilling you? Some research indicates that about 85% of people are involved in careers and jobs they hate. Are you spending your eight hours a day just doing time? What steps are you taking to get into something that will challenge and stimulate your thinking and that will give you a sense of fulfilment?
5. Relationships. What kind of impact do they have in your life? Are these relationships nurturing or toxic? Do they drain you or build you up? These are the questions you should be asking yourself almost daily.

6. Contribution to the world. What are you giving? What will be different in this world because you were born?
So, what kind of a gift are you formulating with your life? Is that how you thank your maker for giving you this gift of life? Think about it!

Horace Mann said, "Be ashamed to die until you have won some victory for humanity."
If you still haven't found that thing that sets your soul on fire, that gives your life a meaning, now is the time to do so.

18. From the ashes, I rise!

"Most men lead lives of quiet desperation and go to the grave with the song still in them. What is called resignation is confirmed desperation"

— Henry David Thoreau

Well, this quote means that most people battle with inexpressible, deep inner struggles nearly impossible to voice. The song within is low and inarticulate. But why this quiet desperation? Thoreau thinks misplaced value is the cause.

We feel a void in our lives and we attempt to fill it with things like money, possessions and accolades.

We think these things will make us happy. When they don't, we seek more of them. The sad reality is that the value we attach to possessions and status is misplaced. Possessions are not the key to happiness, and they may hurt more than they help.

A quote from him I like the most is, "That man is richest whose pleasures are cheapest." The one who enjoys the simplest things in life, is the richest person. Yes, you don't need the most expensive things to be happy, but if you think that way, you are very poor.

This reminds me of the story of a man who had a lot of money but was still not really happy. He decided to buy a much bigger house which would complete his happiness, soon enough, that happiness faded.

He bought another more expensive yacht, and soon enough yet again, the happiness faded. Finally, an idea crossed his mind to donate wheelchairs to the kids who had lost their legs in a war in Bosnia. He got into the chopper with his friend and off they went. They started handing out these wheelchairs, one at a time to these kids. Just before they finished, one boy held his hand tight with tears in his eyes and he wouldn't let go. When asked why he was doing this, he said, "I want to look at your face long enough, to see it well so that I can recognise it in heaven for me to thank you again." These words got this man down on his knees and he was in tears; he felt the joy he had never felt before. That was a turning point of his life, since then, he became a serious philanthropist and lived joyfully.

I am sharing this story to show that joy is not always in receiving but in sharing what you have, especially with the less fortunate. For me, Veli Ndaba, I get so much joy in inspiring and empowering you every week without fail, I am committed to that. What have you committed to in order to make this world a better place?

Yes, when you succeed, you party. When you fail, though, you ponder. All greatness comes from pondering. You must use your force of will to fix your weakest part. You don't want to build your career on your weakest part, but on your strengths. You begin to invest in yourself, study the wisest people, watch YouTube videos of the smart people, and surround yourself with people who are 10 to 20 years ahead of you and with more knowledge than you have. That creates the precision, the skill.

Finally, commit to excellence. The reason most of us go through life never discovering our true greatness is the lack of commitment. The uncommitted life isn't worth living. Why? Because it doesn't produce anything!

Commitment is an interesting thing. When we put ourselves in a situation where we say we're going to do something, it puts you in another zone. When you have that kind of determination, you'll see and experience a positive response all round. Be the man or woman that refuses to be denied.

Yes, you may be feeling down and out right now, feeling hopeless but I would like you to say these words, "From The Ashes, I Rise!"

19. Learn how Mother Nature works

"Nature does not ask your permission, she has nothing to do with your wishes, and whether you like her laws or dislike them, you are bound to accept her as she is, and consequently all her conclusions." — Fyodor Dostoyevsky

Are things happening to you that leave you puzzled? Are bad things happening in your life and you have no idea how to change or control them? Are you enjoying good things and you want to know how to keep it that way? If so, you may want to pay close attention to natural laws. If you pay close attention, you will no longer say, "I don't know why these things happen to me."

We are born into nature and as a result, not following its laws is truly suicidal. Natural laws should be taught in our schools especially in lower grades so as to save us from the pain of colliding with them. You see, Mother Nature is what she is, you take her as she is, she will never play according to your wishes, this you must clearly understand — it's you who must always play according to her rules, call it unfair if you like but hey, it is what it is!

These laws can bring stability, assurance, and confidence to your life if you make the choice of understanding and applying them. Let's look at only three of them:

1. The Law of Relativity

This law states that nothing is what it is until you relate it to something. Point of view is determined by what the observer is relating to.

The nature, value, or quality of something can only be measured in relation to another object. Nothing is good or bad until you relate it to something. In my case, I compared my story of tragically losing my parents at a young age to Les Brown's story of not even knowing his parents. This made me realise how lucky I was to have at least known my parents and to have shared some special moments with them. I felt that my situation wasn't the worst and this gave me hope for the future looking at what he went on to achieve in life in spite of his background.

2. The Law of Cause and Effect

This law states that for every action, there's an equal and opposite reaction. Every cause has an effect, and every effect has a cause. All thought is creative, so be careful of what you wish for... you'll get it. This means whatever you put out there, you'll get it back tenfold. If we have bad thoughts about other people or ourselves, it's going to come back again to us.

Have you ever thought of someone and all of a sudden or soon enough they call you or you bump into them? This proves that our thoughts have magnetic power, what we think about, we bring about!

Say good things to people; treat people with total respect, and it will come back to you. Never worry about what you are going to get. Just concentrate on what you want to give unconditionally. What goes around, comes around.

3. The Law of Gestation

This law states that everything, especially of great value, takes time. All things have a beginning and grow into form as more energy is added to it. Thoughts are like seeds planted in our fertile minds that bloom into our physical experience if we've nourished them. This is something super important to understand. Practice your craft or an idea and do so over and over and over with the appreciation and understanding that in time, it will manifest. Stay focused and know that your goals will become a reality when the time is right.

It's time you stop running away from the highest that is in you. You were born with seeds of greatness, nurture them and protect them with everything you've got.

20. Do you really know what you need?

" You only live once, but if you do it right, once is enough."— Mae West

Yes, the one thing you need to know is that this is your one chance... get out there and live like there is no tomorrow because in the end we really don't know if there will be a tomorrow. This is by no means about being irresponsible, no!

My talks, books and coaching sessions are about self-awareness. If you know yourself, you save yourself from unnecessary pain resulting from wrong pursuits. Knowing yourself, in terms of your strengths, passions, natural abilities is what will help you focus on the right things and make you achieve more while you are enjoying this journey called life.

The worst thing in life is waking up old one day and realising that you became good at the wrong things. The realisation that you focused on the wrong things is one of the worst things that can happen to you. Just imagine mastering the art of procrastinating, complaining, blaming, not taking full responsibility for yourself and holding grudges. These dream killers/distractions take so much of your precious time and energy that you end up having little or no time left to do what you were born to do.

When I spoke to a group of university students who aspire to be entrepreneurs, I emphasised the following important point: "A man was not born just to make his living, but to live his making because living his making will make him a living."

This simply means that you were born to live your making - express your gifts, talents, natural abilities and strengths, this in turn makes you a decent living. To me, Veli Ndaba, the purpose of life is based on: 1. To find your making — who you are and 2. To live your making.

You need to undertake a journey in studying, observing, listening and even asking for feedback from others to understand yourself better, it's a life-time journey, no short cuts. When you understand yourself better you don't get so much entangled in the matrix of life because you're clear of your path.

To summarise what I've said above: The secret to a good living is to do what you HAVE TO as QUICKLY as you can so as to do what you WANT TO for as long as you can. Yes, to those who truly believe, all things are possible!

21. Re-interpret your story

"This is my life...my story...my book. I'll no longer let anyone else write it; nor will I apologize for the edits I make." — Steve Maraboli

You can't start a next chapter of your life if you keep re-reading the last one. You have to learn the lessons from the previous chapters to better your approach for the next coming chapters. Don't let the previous chapter of your story hold you back.

I lost my dad when I was only seven years old, he was brutally stabbed and butchered beyond recognition. My mom died when I was 16 years old — she was knocked down by a car whose driver had been shot dead in a botched hijacking, her body was dragged down the street. My eldest brother was also killed in a mysterious way. I'm not sharing my story for you to feel sorry for me, but to show that there's power in your story and it's up to you on how you use that power.

Whenever things didn't work out well for me, I used my story as the reason and justification for my failure. This, however, changed when I met the one and only Les Brown in 2013 –yes, the world renowned motivational speaker, who became my coach and mentor. When we sat down, he shared his story of not knowing either of his biological parents and indicated how fortunate I was to have known my parents. That, changed my perspective on how I viewed my story.
Whatever happened to you, happened, it can never be changed. The only power you have is to change the interpretation of it to empower you instead of limiting you. As human beings, we're hardwired to act in alignment with how we interpret our story. This means you'll never rise higher than your interpretation of your story which inevitably determine your future.

Reading more stories of men and women who achieved greatness made me realise that my story wasn't a winner. There are many people whose stories are worse than mine, but still, they went on in life to achieve greatness. Dr Viktor Frankl is surely one of them. So, the lesson I learned which I'm certain you'll derive value from it as well, is that you've no control over what happens to you. The control you have, however, is how you interpret that which has happened to you. Your interpretation will either let your story empower you or hinder you from unleashing your greatness.

Your daily behaviour is always a function of your deep beliefs. Your private story — mental narrative — about your potential is the key performance indicator (KPI) on whether you exploit your potential or not.

The positive psychologists call this phenomenon The Self Fulfilling Prophesy, the way we embrace a story about who we are and what we can achieve and then behave in a way that makes that fantasy actually come through.

The world is a mirror and we get from life not what we want, but that which we are. Changing the interpretation of your story will increase your energy and how you show up in the world and this will undoubtedly help you unleash your power!

22. Stop making excuses

"Ninety nine percent of the failures come from people who have the habit of making excuses."
— George Washington Carver

Do you suffer from excusitis? Excusitis is the behaviour of a person that finds all sorts of excuses to justify their poor performance and results, or lack of action. Excuses are the tools of the weak and incompetent used to build monuments of nothingness. Those who excel in it, seldom excel in anything but excuses.

Life has shown us again and again that strength doesn't come from what you can do but from overcoming the things you once thought you couldn't do. As a trained engineer, manager and leader, I never thought I was meant to help people, especially business leaders maximise their results and well- being. But, I always felt that there was more to life and being a curious person, I started searching for that more. When you are curious, you keep moving forward, opening new doors, and doing new things.

Curiosity keeps leading us down new paths. I am always passionately curious. What else can this be? Can you stretch it more? What can happen if I turn this upside down? What new idea can I find in this book? These are but some of the questions I keep asking myself on a daily basis and that's curiosity.

Whatever you make excuses for, you get to keep. In life, you'll never go any higher than you think, that's a fundamental law you need to understand. No matter how old you are now, you are never too young or too old for success or going after what you want. Just think about it:

1. Helen Keller, at the age of 19 months, became deaf and blind. But that didn't stop her. She was the first deaf and blind person to earn a bachelor of arts degree.

2. Mozart was competent on keyboard and violin and composed from the age of 5.

3. John Lennon was 20 years and Paul McCartney was 18 when the Beatles had their first concert in 1961.

4. Nelson Mandela was 76 when he became President.
I can go on and on... The truth is, you are never too young or too old for going after what you want. So, stop making excuses.

I like what Steve Maraboli said, "Your complaints, your drama, your victim mentality, your whining, your blaming, and all of your excuses have NEVER gotten you even a single step closer to your goals or dreams.

Let go of your nonsense. Let go of the delusion that you DESERVE better and go EARN it! Today is a new day!"

Seeking pity, blaming your sad and disadvantaged past will never get you anywhere, I was there myself but it dawned on me that I had the power to live my dreams.
Let today be the day that you choose to be a beacon of hope, that shining example that reminds those who are going through the fiery furnaces of the world that it can be done, in spite of everything.

The world needs you, step up!

23. Failure is the greatest teacher, embrace it!

"Failure is simply the opportunity to begin again, this time more intelligently." — Henry Ford

If you are not willing to learn, no one can help you. But, if you are determined to learn, no one can stop you. You see, destiny is not a matter of chance, it is a matter of choice; it is not a thing to be waited for, it is a thing to be achieved. One of the major ingredients of achievement is failure. Failure itself is not the problem, the problem is how you look at it. Personal development helps you improve your skills and minimise your failures.

The importance of personal development can't be overstated. It's the secret of separating yourself from the pack, the bridge that carries you toward the goals you have yet to reach. Personal development leads you to a place where you feel secure. Feeling secure isn't about knowing you're safe on top of the mountain, it's about trusting in your ability to climb it again if you should fall.

If you were to be dropped on top of the mountain, you won't enjoy much being there because you'll be so worried about falling off — which will mean the end of you.

This is so true with people who are dropped into positions of power and influence without the necessary skills. They never enjoy the role because they spend most of their time protecting themselves from getting dethroned.

They are never settled because they know that once they're dethroned, it's all over with them, they'll never come back. So, they are never trusting, not because people can't be trusted, but because they don't trust themselves, they end adopting bullying techniques and they never listen or take other people's inputs or advices. You see, this is not about the outside world, but the inner one. Your outside world is an expression of an inner world.

This quote succinctly explains this, "A bird sitting on a tree is never afraid of the branch breaking, because her trust is not on the branch, but on its own wings. Always believe in yourself" — Unknown. So, a bird that doesn't believe in itself, simply relies on the branch. If the branch breaks, it goes down with it, I'm certain you get what I'm saying here. You can't rely on a leadership position to fix things, you need better ideas and influence, not just positional power.

We spend a lot of time investing in things that numb us to the reality of how short life is—things like scrolling the internet and our cell phones for hours on end, or watching TV to the point of restlessness. Entertainment is fun, but how much time do we save for ourselves?

How often do we set aside dedicated time for personal reflection and prayer, where we are learning and growing in a way that defines our existence?

Life is growth. If we stop growing, technically and spiritually, we are as good as dead. One of my mentors liked to say, "Losers visualise the penalties of failure. Winners visualise the rewards of success."

I think this is mainly so because we are socialised to believe and think that failure is the worst thing in the world, you fail because you're stupid. Failure is therefore associated with stupidity and as a result, it has to be avoided at all cost. So, many people give up on their dreams before they even get started because there's a possibility of failure and appearing stupid, how sad.

Muhammad Ali said, "You don't lose if you get knocked down; you lose if you stay down." These are the words I live by. I get knocked down so many times in my life but one thing for sure about me, I stubbornly refuse to stay down. Every failure presents another opportunity for me to begin again more intelligently each time, so, I fail forward toward my dreams!

24. Set yourself apart

"If a man can write a better book or preach a better sermon or make a better mousetrap than his neighbour, even if he builds his house in the woods, the world will make a beaten path to his door."

— Ralph Waldo Emerson

These words simply mean that if you can do something better than other people around you, not just those in your neighbourhood, even though you live somewhere remote and hard to get to, people will put in a lot of effort to get to you. Specifically, this refers to making a path through the wood, often done by beating down the shrubs and plants until they can be walked over.

In every field you can ever think of, there is what is called a hierarchy of competence. This is a pyramid, the top of it is occupied by masters (about five percent or so) and below that is just the rest. The rest is made out of good, just good, average, less than average and incompetent. What really separates the top from the bottom ones, I hear you ask? Well, to me, the main reasons for one not to reach the top are:

1. Chasing too many rabbits or

2. Chasing the wrong rabbit

Chasing too many rabbits means that you never get to catch one. trying to be good at everything means that you never get to be exceptionally good in one thing. It's good to be multi-skilled, yet you need to — at some stage — focus on one thing that can set you apart from everyone else.

Chasing the wrong rabbit is like unrequited love, it's hell. All you do is spend your days thinking and chasing someone who will never think of you nor chase you back. You'd do anything for that person, and they'll do nothing for you.

Someone once said that unrequited love is like waiting for an airplane at a train station. This is choosing a wrong career, the one not suited to your highest strength, and staying at the bottom of that career's hierarchy for the rest of your working life.

25. Always keep these two windows open

"Keep your face to the sunshine and you cannot see a shadow."— *Helen Keller*

Keeping one's face to the sunshine is a metaphor for maintaining a positive, optimistic outlook on life. And what Keller is saying is that maintaining a positive, optimistic attitude to life is the best way to avoid being overtaken by negative, pessimistic thoughts. Light is crucial for us as it comes from our Creator. There's an old Biblical blessing that says, "May the Lord make His face shine upon you." (Numbers 6:24-26) To let in the light, you need to open some windows. The two critical windows that you want to always keep open are:

1.   Window of Hope
2.   Window of Opportunity

1. Window of Hope
This window is so critical that you have to do whatever it takes to keep it open because everything else depends on it. Once this window closes on you, darkness takes over.

Darkness is about doom and gloom, hopelessness, helplessness, victimhood and so on and so forth. When this window is opened, you keep seeing possibilities of good things, your self-worth, that your life counts and that it doesn't matter how long it takes but eventually, through your deliberate persistence, it will come to pass. Constant motivation (intrinsic and extrinsic) keeps this hope alive even when all seems impossible. You don't want your life to be overtaken by negative thoughts.

We are always exposed to negative news on TV, radio, social media networks, people and print media and the best for you is to avoid these as much as possible and instead feed your mind with positive thoughts andmessages. It's impossible to thrive in the world of rapid change and insane interconnectedness without building an effective defence perimeter around your mind. Jim Rohn said it well: "Every Day Stand Guard At The Door Of Your Mind". Optimism is the faith that leads to any achievement. Nothing can be done without hope and confidence in yourself.

2.   Window of Opportunity
Tom Peters said, "If the window of opportunity appears, don't pull down the shade." This window is about taking action at the right time. It's about seizing the moment. Thousands of people attend classes, seminars, conferences, workshops thus receiving some brilliant ideas and coaching on the important things to do. But guess what, they never act on that information. It seems like people attend these events just to collect expensive notebooks.

You see, knowledge not applied will never give you power. Having knowledge without acting on it in the right time will never work for you. Always keep your eyes and mind open to opportunities; they are always there for you to take advantage of — if you notice them.

Your dreams have long been calling you, it's time to pick up and answer the call! You want your child, brother, sister, mom, friend to be the best they can be, don't you? So too your Creator wants you to be the best you can be. Keep those windows open!

26. Be careful about your environment

"Sow a thought, and you reap an act; Sow an act, and you reap a habit; Sow a habit, and you reap a character; Sow a character, and you reap a destiny."
— Samuel Smiles

When any habit has been well formed by repetition of thought and action, the mind attaches itself to and follows that habit as closely as possible. When a habit has been well formed it becomes a force which in due course, will regulate an individual's life.

It has been well said that "all men are the creatures of habit." This means a habit is a cable; we weave a thread of it each day and it becomes so strong that we cannot break it. Warren Buffet said, "Chains of habit are too light to be felt until they are too heavy to be broken."

Once a habit is well formed, it becomes a cruel tyrant, it rules and compels a person to act against their will and desires.

The good news though is that this mighty force can be harnessed and set to work for us, instead of being slave to it and serving it faithfully (though complaining). To harness or control it, you first need to understand its fundamental principles.

A habit is a mental path over which our actions have travelled for some time, each passing making the path a little deeper and a little wider.
If you have to walk over a field or through a forest, you know how natural it is for you to choose the clearest path in preference to the less treaded ones. It all starts with a thought and the question we should ask ourselves is, "How and what feeds our thoughts?" Well, our thoughts are fed by the surrounding environment. The term 'environment' covers a very broad field.

Environment consist of books we read, the people with whom we associate, the community in which we live, the lifestyle in which we are engaged, the country or nation in which we reside and most important of all, the religion and intellectual training we receive prior to the age of 14. The importance of analysing the subject of environment is to show its direct relationship to the personality we are developing. The mind feeds upon that which we supply it, or that which is forced upon it, through our environment.

Therefore, let every positive individual select their environment, as far as possible, with the intention of supplying the mind with suitable materials which will help make them a success in life. If your environment is not to your liking, change it, you've the power to do so!

Your daily associates, that is, the people you meet and move with constitute one of the most important and influential parts of your environment, and may work for your progress or your retrogression, according to the nature of those associations. Remember that every word spoken within your hearing, everything that reaches your eyes, and every sense impression that you receive through any of the five senses, influences your thought as surely as the sun rises in the east and sets in the west.
Now, you can see the power of your environment and how your thoughts are fed. You can now see the importance of reading books that deal with subjects which are directly related to your dreams and quality of life. Can you now see the importance of talking with people who are in sympathy with your aims and who will encourage you and spur you on toward your visions and aspirations?

So, be very careful about your surrounding environment, it has the unbelievable power to nourish your thoughts with either a superior quality or substandard materials that will ultimately make you the person you'll become.

27. Commitment produces mastery

So, there's magic when you commit to something, especially greatness. Committing is when you say, "I'll do whatever it takes, no matter what." Once you commit, you'll find dazzling miracles. You get to see the things, people and situations you wouldn't ordinarily see. I've personally achieved so much through this process. Until you commit to greatness, things will not fall into place, period. It's not about you getting better things, but you getting better! Commitment consists of the following three elements:

1. What you said you'll do;
2. When you said you'll do it;
3. Whether you feel like it or not.

I recently had a conversation with my 17-year-old son to explain and take him through these steps. So, commitment is doing what you said you would do, when you said you would do It, whether you feel like it or not.
I committed to writing weekly articles for a newspaper publication and Linkedin platform every Sunday before 12pm.

I committed to writing two whatsapp status updates to inspire and empower others, every day by 8am. I committed to do physical exercise for a minimum of three days a week.

I committed to personally call a minimum of five people a day to let them know how unique and special they are. These I do every day whether I like it or not.
What I've learnt through this is that willpower and courage are developed when you engage the third element of commitment - Doing it whether you like it or not! This has hugely contributed to the person I'm today. Every day when I wake up I ask myself a question, "Veli, what is commitment?" Then, I read the three elements out loud! This gives me a kick!!! What are your main commitments? I would guess that your commitments revolve around your Creator, your well-being, your family and your work.

What Steve Jobs said about work shook me to the core, so let me share it with you: "Your work is going to fill a large part of your life, and the only way to be truly satisfied is to do what you believe is great work. And the only way to do great work is to love what you do. If you haven't found it yet, Keep looking. Don't settle. As with all the matters of the heart, you'll know when you find it. And, like any great relationship, it just gets better as the years roll on. So keep looking until you find it. Don't settle."

After hearing that I didn't rest until I 'found' my great work. May it do the same with you.

I invite you to reflect even further: "Any guy can love a thousand girls, but only a rare guy can love one girl in a thousand ways," said Dr Karl Menninger. This to me means that it's easy to be a jack of all trades, to love thousand things but it takes high level of self-awareness, passion, discipline, dedication, faith and patience to love and do one thing well albeit a thousand times, whether you feel like it or not.

So, be that rare guy or girl that commits to greatness, immerses in greatness and delivers greatness day in and day out.

28. In life, everything has an opportunity cost

"The opportunity cost of an unlived dream is not only that dream, but also the dreams the dream was meant to inspire." — Ryan Lilly

In economics, opportunity cost means the loss of other alternatives when one alternative is chosen. When an option is chosen from alternatives, the opportunity cost is the "cost" incurred by not enjoying the benefit associated with the best alternative choice. Idle cash balances represent an opportunity cost in terms of interest.

Life is all about values and priorities, you face trade-offs. Life always requires of you to make choices among mutually exclusive alternatives. Every time you select something, you forfeit other alternatives and associated benefits. The cost of something is what you will give up to get it.

You can do anything but not everything and therefore, the question you are always faced with is, what will you sacrifice when you choose one option over the others?

Even more critical is your knowledge or awareness of the options with their associated benefits that you're giving up! This is when doing your homework is key, not just rushing things up without evaluating the available alternatives.

Well, I believe that thinking in terms of opportunity cost is the best way to approach life. It's based on the fact that when you use your scarce resources like time, money and energy for something, you miss the opportunity to use it for something else that may yield better results. The value of that something else is the cost that you have to pay. With this concept in mind, it's simple to see whether you use your scarce resources effectively.

The problem is that it's easy to spend your time without thinking about the opportunity cost. It's easy to just follow the path of least resistance and do what feels good at the moment. While it might make you feel good now, it won't help you realise your full potential.

We live in a world of scarcity and must therefore make choices. You cannot avoid regret since there are opportunity costs for every choice you will make. Every time you say "yes" to a choice, you are also saying "no" to everything else you may have otherwise accomplished with your time, money, and other resources. Opportunity cost is a commanding tool that you should be wise to apply to all decision-making. If you integrate this concept into your thought process, you will not only make wise choices, but also better understand the world in which you live.

Whether you are choosing a career path or switching from one to another, starting a business, investing your money, buying a car, or throwing away your evening watching TV, considering the value of lost alternatives will help you make better decisions. Make the lens of opportunity costs the underpinning of your decision-making processes.

Once again, please get this to yourself, "The opportunity cost of an unlived dream is not only that dream, but the dreams that dream was meant to inspire." This is so profound in that you are not only responsible for your own dreams, but other people's (alive and unborn) dreams that depend on yours. So, every time you misuse your time, you are throwing your potential and dreams away — and not only do you do that, but also, you are throwing away other people's dreams people who would have been inspired and encouraged by yours. Not living your dream is a great loss!

You can maximise your potential by keeping in mind opportunity cost moment-by-moment, it is not difficult. Before doing an activity, any activity, ask yourself, "Is this the best use of my time?" "What else could I do with this time?" For instance, you might be thinking of spending the evening binge- watching a TV show or anything of that sort. But here you should stop and ask yourself, "Is this the best use of my time?" "What else could I best use this time for?" You might come up with other ideas such as reading a book, working on a side project or learning a new skill. Remember, your uniqueness is what makes you special, don't waste it. You have the power to live your dreams!

29. Success is a very tricky fellow

"Success means doing the best we can with what we have. Success is the doing, not the getting; in the trying, not the triumph. Success is a personal standard, reaching for the highest that is in us, becoming all that we can be." — Zig Ziglar

Success is a very tricky and naughty fellow, it likes and enjoys playing hide and seek and hiding behind and inside disappointments and failures. So, if you're not willing to embrace disappointments and failures and appear a fool at times, you can kiss it goodbye!Therefore, in order to achieve your goals and dreams, you have to be prepared to be seriously tested and to fail with grace. How you handle disappointments and failures counts towards your journey to greatness. That's one important muscle you need to develop in life: how to handle failures and awkward situations.

As you step out today, don't let any disappointment and failure stop you from claiming your stuff! It's time that you snatch that victory from the jaws of defeat!

Come on, you can do this!

30. What can I learn from this?

"All men make mistakes, but only wise men learn from their mistakes." — Winston Churchill

We've all been through sad and embarrassing situations, this is part of who we become in life. But one thing you must not do, is letting that sad and embarrassing past define your future. You are much better than your past. Whenever you share your sad story, never share it from a place of weakness, helplessness or victimhood. Tell it from a place of power, pride and courage, however sad or embarrassing it may be. Let your scars remind you of your power and resilience and let it be a great example to teach others that they, too, can do it. That's how I turned my life around, just by adopting this approach! It's a critical and learnable skill one needs to develop.

We all have sad stories. When you hear other people's stories, you soon realise that you were all along under the wrong impression that your sad story is the saddest ever. You may have used it as an excuse for your weakness and for beating yourself over and over.

You can't change your story, but you have the power to change the interpretation of it. Don't focus solely on what happened, instead, ask yourself this question, "What's the good thing/s I can learn from this story/setback?" That will help you claim your power back! What's your take?

31. Optimism, a noble trait that sets you apart!

"Attitude is a choice. Happiness is a choice. Optimism is a choice. Kindness is a choice. Giving is a choice. Respect is a choice. Whatever choice you make makes you. Choose wisely."— Roy T. Bennet

Optimism is hopefulness and confidence about the future or the success of something. Being an optimist doesn't require life to be a bed of roses, or that you have an amazing childhood or that your life is already wonderful. The truth is, we are all in a gutter of some sort at any given time. As I write this, our gutter is the COVID-19 pandemic, this crisis sees no colour, gender, race, creed, country, etc. as it affects everyone who is alive right now on planet earth. You see, we're all in a gutter, but the difference is that some of us are looking at the stars. Looking at the stars makes you focus on the bright side of things, obviously not ignoring the dark side but choosing to focus on the bright side and that's what optimism is all about. I always bring science into my talks, writings and thinking to back up my message.

Optimism is a fundamental way we communicate with ourselves. For a long time, people believed that what humans had been conditioned to be is who we'd become and we couldn't change that. But then in 1965, Dr Martin Seligman — who is known to be one of the leading researchers in the field of positive psychology (Pennsylvania University) — came out and said "No, no! We can actually shape the way we show up."

Dr Seligman came to that conclusion after he and Dr Steven Maier had conducted an experiment on three sets of dogs. After these experiments where electric shock was applied on two sets of dogs (the first set of dogs had no means to escape; the second had means and the third set was in a controlled environment — no electric shock applied). The last experiment, where the conditions of the environment had been changed so that all the dogs could run away from the shocks but when the shocks were applied as in previous experiments, the first set of dogs just crawled up into a ball in the corner, and continued to suffer the shocks.

This is how learned helplessness theory was formed. So, learned helplessness is a behaviour exhibited by a subject after enduring repeated unpleasant stimuli beyond their control. This is when people accept their powerlessness, discontinuing attempts to escape or avoid the aversive or unfavourable situation even when the alternatives are clearly presented. Martin Seligman said, "One of the most important findings in psychology in the last 20 years is that individuals can choose the way they think." This means that if you can learn pessimism, you can also learn optimism. This led to his theory called Learned Optimism.

Learned Optimism is more about changing the fundamental way we communicate with ourselves. If you haven't noticed, we're always talking to ourselves in our heads and he called that 'explanatory style'. This consists of the way you think about setbacks and the way you think about victories in your life.

Optimistic persons, when they have a setback, believe that it's temporary and that they can change it. Pessimistic persons believe the same setback is permanent, it's going to last forever!

Conversely, when a victory occurs, the optimistic person embraces it and believes it's permanent. The optimistic person believes he deserves it and uses the victory as an aid in other circumstances. The pessimistic person on the other hand, shrugs it off and says, "I didn't do it, it's just a once-off situation and it's just going to help me in this domain of my life."

Techniques on how to change your explanatory style — from pessimistic to optimistic orientation, using cognitive therapy developed by Steven Hollon and Arthur Freeman, you firstly need to identify the ABC's:

- Adversity that is encountered.
- Beliefs that arise (what you think).
- Consequences (what you do).

Initially you simply record what happens. Then use the following techniques to deal with your pessimistic beliefs once you are aware of them:

1. Distract yourself when they occur - try to think of something else.

2. Dispute them. Disputing is more effective in the long run, because successfully disputed beliefs are less likely to recur when the same situation presents itself again.

Now, you can start to watch and notice yourself to identify your dominant orientation and start applying the above techniques and in time you'll learn to take control of your thoughts and become more optimistic, make wise choices and unleash your greatness! If you believe in prayer, go into prayer when you feel your pessimism rise inside you and humbly ask God to renew your mind so you can see the good and not stay stuck in the bad and the sad.

As much as you learned helplessness, you can also learn optimism. You've now seen through your life's experiences that helplessness doesn't at all help you achieve your dreams, but rather renders you a victim. Now, it's your time to switch to positive mode and live your dreams!

32. Excellence is a process not an event!

"I start early and I stay late, day after day, year after year; it took me 17 years and 114 days to become an overnight success." — Lionel Messi

It's very interesting that people are so quick to identify overnight successes. You hear them say, "Wow, things just happen for him/her, he/she's just a natural." They don't seem to get real and see beyond the results — the hard work, the pain, the tears, the patience and the sacrifices made behind the scenes. Until you realise that trophies are won at practice and only collected at competitions, you'll never be a so-called "overnight success".

It may take a day for people to notice when the lights come on and shine on you and envy the excellence. Rather than focusing and envying a person who displays excellence, focus on what they do behind the scenes and replicate it.

You have the seeds of excellence in you, water and grow them!

33. Two bloody wars towards your dreams!

"Desire! That's the one secret of every man's career. Not education. Not being born with hidden talents. Desire."
— Johnny Carson

Fighting for your dreams will introduce you to pain, challenges, doubters, mistakes, unfavourable feedback and of course, hard work. Fighting for your dreams requires you to thrive in solitude because that's how you can connect with that deep, constant voice that is your true guide and shining light to your destiny.

Fighting for your dreams means trusting in your vision when the world calls you crazy. It is the clear understanding that success is not something that's divinely bestowed on you, it's something you earn by having a clear vision, grit, hard work, adaptability and surrounding yourself with the right people. The world is not yet a crazy enough place to reward a bunch of undeserving people. I am mentioning adaptability here because it's quite key in your fighting. Adaptability helps you see when the target has shifted from where it initially was.

Adaptability is intelligence that you need to build into your fighting recipe especially in this ever changing world of ours, call it VUCA (Volatile, Uncertain, Complex and Ambiguous) world.

This is, by the way, the topic I'll be speaking on at the 2020 Africa CEO RoundTable — How To Lead In The VUCA World.

I remember a conversation I had with my mentor Les Brown in 2014 around this subject of fighting for your dreams. He said to me, "Veli, when you're fighting for your dreams, you'll lose friends, you'll be misunderstood and called names. Doors of opportunities will be shut in your face not because you are not good at what you do, but because of decision-makers who don't know better." He further said, "Don't let that make you doubt your abilities, no! Don't take it personally, it's entirely not your fault. Yours is to keep fighting for your dreams and continue being an instrument of hope and service that you are." These words have kept me growing through difficult situations. I've learnt so much in this speaking, coaching and consulting journey and about life in general.

One of the most important lessons I've learnt is to not blindly focus on the end goal, but also to be aware of the person I'm becoming in pursuing that goal. You may fight for something that makes you a bitter, angry, greedy, impatient person and that's not good for you. So, be careful of the person you are becoming while you're pursuing your goals and dreams, some may be toxic to you.

What drives you to achieve your dreams is desire. Your desire to succeed in whatever you do, determines your level of motivation. It is your burning desire that makes you win these two bloody wars. Which wars am I talking about here? Well, here they are:

Winning yourself over from other people's expectations, limitations and opinions of you. This is to become your own person. To choose your own path and run it at your own pace. Ralph Waldo Emerson said, "To be yourself in a world that is constantly trying to make you something else is the greatest accomplishment." This is the first tough bloody war. It's a pity that most people never conquer this war, they just give in and go with the flow.

Fighting for your dreams and career. Dreams are so hard to follow and achieve but don't let anyone, I mean anyone, take them away from you. Oh! I like what Mark Sullivan said, "To find a career to which you are adapted by nature, and then work so hard at it, is about as near to a formula for success and happiness as the world provides." This second bloody war involves figuring out your natural abilities — your life's task — and work hard at it. Mine is speaking, writing and coaching, being an instrument of hope and service. This is what I do every day with a huge smile on my face! What is your life's task that keeps you going every day?

To win this second bloody war, you need to develop a culture of High Performance. Here are some of the ingredients for high performance that I teach individuals and organisations:

1. Set a clear goal/expectation;

2. Develop competence on achieving the set goal;

3. Commit to the set goal. Commitment is doing what you said you'll do, when you said you'll do it whether you like or not. Commit to your commitments.

4. Create a supportive climate to achieve your goal. You need to surround yourself with people that are as hungry as you are and that will also call you on your stuff when you slack. This will create a great environment for success.

Your dreams are calling you and always know that you deserve them. You deserve the best that life has to offer, claim it!

34. Weaponise your beliefs

"Believe that life is worth living and your belief will help create the fact." — William James

In the Toltec tradition, they make a differentiation between people who are 'artists' and people who are the 'canvas'. So, the artist paint the masterpiece of their life, they hold the brush, they decide how they want to make themselves, they basically forge themselves. These people decide how they want to be and how they want to show up in life.

Then, on the other side are the people who are constantly getting paint splattered on them by other people telling them what they should be. These people swallow everything they are told to do and to be. Oh, you should be this or that; you should do this or should do that; you need to look like this and dress like that. These people are constantly being shaped by external pressure.

You see, in life you either conform to these external pressures and expectations or you say, "No, No, No! I don't take that, I'm the artist, I'll decide what I accept."

You can make your beliefs work for you instead of them working against you — this is weaponising your beliefs. This is using your healthy and supportive beliefs to propel you towards your good and desired life.

Remember, a belief is a strong feeling you have about something, right or wrong. It's possible to feel very strong about something wrong and fight for it with everything you have to protect it and whatever you protect or fight for, you get to keep. Now, it's time to let go of the beliefs that are working against your desires of elevating your life. The first step to achieving this is to acknowledge that you've been a victim of this self-sabotage all along. You have to accept that you've been a canvas instead of being the artist of your life.

Step 1: Forgive yourself for what happened in the past and understand that you're not the same person you were then. You're now the person that has learned from all those past mistakes.

Step 2: Fast forward where you are today. Look at yourself in 10, 15 and 20 years' time and ask yourself this question, "Is that what I want to be?" And if the answer is "No!" Then, you need to find a new path. You need to understand yourself more by raising your level of self-awareness that will lead you to self-mastery. You don't know what you need in your life until you figure out who you are.

Step 3: You need to learn and understand why our conditioned beliefs affect our ability to achieve our potential, you need to know something about the conscious and subconscious elements of your mind.

You need to understand that the subconscious mind is like a plot of fertile soil, whatever is sown, it will grow. If our subconscious was negatively conditioned throughout our childhood, this is highly likely to be the reason why we do not achieve or use our full potential.

Imagine for a moment a baby elephant fastened to a pole outside a circus tent. In the beginning, he tries to move away, but only succeeds in hurting himself. After a while, he gives up trying. When he grows up to become a large elephant fastened to exactly the same pole, he will continue to walk around it even though he is capable of trampling down the entire circus tent. This is exactly what happens with the beliefs which have been conditioned in us.

Although we have been designed by the Creator to be winners, most of us have been conditioned to become losers. This conditioning has affected our self-belief to such an extent that it actually restricts us from utilising our full potential.

Step 4: Say positive affirmations. As mentioned above, if the subconscious is fed negativity, our lives will be full of negativity, together with self-critical behaviour and negative self-perceptions. A positive affirmation is a statement which is repeated time and time again, so that it becomes a belief and the mind convinces the body to conform to this belief.

When you do this, you'll begin to see how positive you become and will appreciate the clarity in your life. You were truly born to win, cleanse your mind of negative beliefs and claim your power!

35. Major sources of inspiration

"If a man does not keep pace with his companions, perhaps it is because he hears a different drummer. Let him step to the music which he hears, however measured or far away." — *Henry David Thoreau*

Many people have a lot of missed calls in their lives simply because of the noise around them. This noise has drowned and deafened the voice that is meant to guide and lead them to their destiny. Yes, it seems that the opposite of courage in our world today is not cowardice any more, but conformity. To be truly yourself in this world that is so well set up to make you conform is a great accomplishment.

To be able to step to the beat of a different drummer as opposed to that heard by the masses, takes a lot of faith and trust in yourself. You have to know that you are different, unique, special and that you were created to be solution to a particular problem in this world. The reason I, Veli Ndaba, was born was to remind you of your purpose and to help you reconnect with the highest that's within you.

When you were conceived, a seed of greatness was planted in you and yours is to protect it, water it, cultivate it, fertilise it and remove unwanted weeds around it until it is harvest time. To achieve this, you need to stay inspired. When you are truly inspired, the word 'IMPOSSIBLE' becomes 'I'M POSSIBLE'.

Successful people don't become that way overnight. What most people see at a glance — happiness, wealth, a great career, purpose — is the result of belief and faith, dedication, persistence and of course, adaptability. These people develop a miracle mindset and I speak a lot around this concept on different platforms. So, they believe in themselves and their dreams and become expectant. Here's how to immerse yourself in these sources of inspiration for you to stay inspired:

Step1: Deciding what to do — most people suffer from indecision, they never take a decision. A decision is a culmination of a process that starts with a need to decide. It's then followed by the deciding process where brain-storming possible decisions happens and so on. This is the process that I unpack. Taking a decision inspires you because it then becomes clearer what you need to do next.

Step2: Planning how to do it — this is when you look at the how, when, who and resources required, etc. Unfortunately most people and even businesses never do justice to this process. Critical things and steps are overlooked. You've heard of the saying that failing to plan, is planning to fail. Planning helps you know how to go about what it is you decided to do and this inspires you to carry on.

Step 3: Beginning to do it — this now helps you put everything in motion. Starting has magic in it. When you see what you decided to do and planned getting in motion — whoa! that's huge, believe you me.

This inspires you and shows you that you are on the right track. This also gives you the opportunity to fine tune whatever needs fine tuning. You see, you cannot steer a stationary vehicle let alone make a U-turn, it has to be in motion.

Step 4: Progressing — this is when you see yourself taking baby-steps. For me, building my speaking career for example was an exciting journey. Seeing myself planning, receiving coaching and delivering that CC1 (level 1) speech at my Toastmasters club. Next time doing the same thing for my CC2 speech until my CC10 (level 10) speech. Inspiration comes as a result of feeling a sense of control and progress.

Step 5: Achieving — This is when you reach your intended and desired destination. This is when you feel the sense of achieving your goal.

This process of staying inspired doesn't focus on what you finally get, but rather on who you become along the journey, which is very important. This is how character is built, it's a process not an event.

I trust this helps you like it helps me achieve my goals and dreams. You have the power to live your dreams!

36. How to re-invent yourself

"People who have had little self-reflection live life in a huge reality blind spot." — Bryant McGill

Everything in your life is a reflection of a choice you have made. If you want a different result, make a different choice. Self-reflection is truly a humbling process. It's essential to find out why you think, say, and do certain things so that you can go on to improve yourself.

Like the sand through the hour glass, so are the days of our lives. Like the candle in the wind, soon, you and I will be gone forever. I was born to remind you that you are a solution to a certain problem in the world and also to help you quieten the noise around you in order to hear your soft inner voice that is meant to guide and lead you to your greatness. For you not to be trapped inside the happenings of life, here's the 'formula' that has saved me by keeping me awake. I have no doubt it will benefit you as well. Start by reflecting:

1. What did I plan? Write those things down

2. What did I achieve and what did I not?

Write them down
3. What did I do to achieve what I did? Write them down.
4. What didn't I do for me not to achieve what I had planned?
These are the first practical reflection questions in whatever situation you are dealing with. Now, the following second set of questions should follow once you've completed the first.

1. What must I do more of? Here, you want to double or increase what works — beliefs, thoughts, habits, behaviour, etc.
2. What must I do less of? This is to help you minimise your effort on what is no longer contributing much.
3. What must I stop altogether? This is to help you crush or fold what isn't working any more. This is to help you re-channel your time and energies onto something else instead of wasting time on what is no longer adding value in your life.
4. What must I introduce to improve my results and life as a whole? This will help you stay relevant by re-inventing yourself and by continually honing your skills, keep you growing and excited.

For me, this is the best gift I can give you. My talks, coaching sessions and books are all around the idea of self-awareness and unleashing your greatness. So, if you really want to raise the bar in your life, you now know what to do, just follow the steps above and add your own flavour along the way and you will see and experience your life transforming.

You have the power to live your dreams.

37. Being specific improves mental clarity

"I always wanted to be somebody, but now I realize I should have been more specific."
— Lily Tomlin

Specificity, or the act of being specific, allows you to know exactly what you want. It might not help you with every decision, but it will help in some of the key decisions, if you can ask which choice will get you closer to your very specific outcome.

When you are specific, you won't become a wondering generality, as Zig Ziglar would nicely put it. Be specific when you set goals. I've learnt in life that achieving goals is important, but the person you become in achieving those goals is even more important. I need to state upfront that you won't achieve every goal you set out to achieve but the experiences you'll have, will set you apart and get you at a higher level of consciousness.
I would like to share with you the method that I use to set and achieve goals. I've also adopted it in my coaching

and consulting interventions. I'll give you a high level approach here just to get you started.

1. Identify the GOAL you want to achieve. Let's say: a good public speaker.

2. Identify Strategies, Methods, Process. STRATEGY is a WHAT you need to do to achieve your goal. Read books on public speaking and practice it. METHOD is a HOW you will do it — Get a mentor/coach, join a Toastmasters club near you, etc.
   PROCESS is a system you'll use in executing your HOWs. This is how you schedule your activities in a day.

3. Write down the BEHAVIOUR required for you to execute and achieve the above, this is about the disciplines you need to have. Self-awareness is key here. Understand your habit loop. Your habits drive your behaviour.

4. What BELIEFS must you hold true for you to have the behaviour required. This is important to know because your behaviour is driven by your beliefs. You may want to achieve a hundred but if you only believe that you are only capable of achieving fifty, then you will be out of sync with your goal. This is where doubt comes in and sabotages your goals. You firstly need to believe that you are worthy and capable of achieving your goal, it's a journey not an event.

5. What is your BIG WHY/s? This is reason/s you want to achieve your goal. I always liken the WHY to fire and heat. Small fire produces small heat and big consistent fire produces big heat.

So, the size or strength of your WHY determines your resilience and persistence, that 'I'll do whatever it takes' attitude.

When the above are in order, there's ALIGNMENT or COHERENCE. This means your GOAL, BEHAVIOUR, BELIEFS are all in agreement and that's what leads to goal achievement. You need to challenge yourself by setting goals that will make you feel uncomfortable, your potential lies outside of your comfort zone. It's true that most people don't fail in life because they aim to high and miss, but that they aim too low and hit. Setting and achieving lousy goals doesn't bring out the best in you, it doesn't push you to the next level of your potential.

We are raised and socialised to believe and act in certain ways. We operate within the constraints of the dominant society and the things that they've created for us and it's a serious challenge to see yourself beyond that and to work to get outside of that even after the things have changed because that has become so much part of you. You unconsciously operate within the parameters of what has been put in place. For you to get out requires a conscious deliberate determination to firstly think outside of what life has thrown at you.

When we are specific about our goals, we become very clear of the journey ahead and the focus gets to be channelled where it matters most. When you watch lions attacking a group buffaloes or zebras, they don't just chase after the pack, they identify just one in a pack and stick with it until the end and more often than not, they catch it.

Being specific helps you effectively focus your energies on the most important things. Be stubborn about your goals, but be flexible about your methods. Yes, specificity will help you become that somebody you've always wanted to become.

38. How do you know
you are off the mark?

*"The archer who misses his mark does not blame the target. He stops, corrects himself
and shoots again."* — Confucius

If you need external stimulus or outside things to complete you, you are off the mark my friend.
When you find yourself constantly wanting this and that because they'll make you feel recognised and complete.
When you find yourself often saying I need this because once I have it (things like)- fame, money, big-screen tv, Netflix, video games, etc, I'll feel complete. It's ok to have these things but they shouldn't determine your completeness. They're just resources to numb you from the pains and miseries of the world and keep you from doing the real stuff.

True joy, serenity and internal fulfilment is what you should strive for, it's the real stuff!

External stimuli or resources should help you further your course in life, not numb you. They should act as enablers for you and others that you can help rather than them becoming a disadvantage to you.

Acquiring resources shouldn't be the end to your means, but your means to an end. What's your take on this?

39. You are the architect
of your future!

"It's not enough to be in the right place at the right time, you must be the right person in the right place at the right time." — T. Harv Eker

The way you see yourself in the future is what determines your level of motivation today. If you see yourself as worthy and better off than what you are now, you'll be driven to close the gap. You'll be eager to develop yourself and work harder on improving your skills to match that future image.

So, self-image is quite key in how you show up every day. If your future self-image is fuzzy, low or just more or less the same as today's, developing yourself won't make any sense to you because that won't match up with you future self — in other words you won't have anything great to strive for.

You can be advised, encouraged and even be presented with the best opportunities in the world but until those opportunities match up with how you see yourself in the future, they won't make any sense.

There are two kinds of people in the world: those who let things happen to them (keeping their fingers crossed and hoping for the best) and those who make things happen for themselves. Which one of the two have you chosen to be?

40. Why winners should quit!

"Winners never quit and quitters never win."
— Vince Lombard

Growing up has taught me so many things especially the power of effective questions. Had I not changed and upgraded my perspective on life, I would continue taking things at face value. There are so many people that are stuck because they just take things that are said at face value without really questioning them and understanding the proper context. I decided today just to share two of these things which are very popular motivational sayings or clichés.

We've all heard the old adage, "Winners never quit and quitters never win." Is that really true and if so, in what context? Why is it that in jobs and businesses people often believe that if they just persist, somehow things will get better? And that they need to be loyal and never show signs of "giving up"?

Now, let me say this upfront. To me, winners do not quit or give up because the task is difficult, they quit because it won't yield the desired results. Winners should sometimes quit — and quit quickly. Yes, I know we hear that quote about nothing matters but persistence, but if you're a duck trying to climb a tree, all persistence will get you is web feet that are too sore to even swim. Have the maturity and guts to quit the wrong things in your life. Don't let the commonly accepted clichés misdirect you from the unique path you are on.

Do you remember what Albert Einstein said, "Everybody is a genius. But if you judge a fish by its ability to climb a tree, it will live its whole life believing it is stupid." There are many people who are so frustrated and believing they are stupid because of wrongly measuring their abilities. The world can be such a cruel and cold place when it comes to measuring people's abilities. You need to pause and study yourself in order to learn about your true abilities. You hold the master key in this, you are the one that feels whatever you feel inside of you and you and you alone can honestly study your past and pick up the patterns of your strengths and passions. You have the responsibility to correct this situation.

The second cliché is, "You can do anything you set or put your mind to." Once again, this sounds too unrealistic to me. A lack of self-awareness will definitely let you down here because you are likely to set you set yourself up for failure and frustration. This is more like unrequited love. All you do is spend your days thinking of someone who will never think of you. This kind of love hurts, it is like waiting for an aeroplane at a train station.

What really makes winners keep on winning? Well, to me it's mainly the following:

1. They truly understand the value and importance on limited resources. Time, money and energy — willpower. They know very well that they only have so much of them, you lose them, they are gone! They are always looking for the optimal/best way of investing them. They are not loyal to things that don't work hence they quit.

2. They cut their losses. They are good at abandoning a course that is clearly going to be unprofitable or unsuccessful before they suffer more losses or harm. You hear people saying, "Well, I've already invested a lot here and it will be pointless for me to give up." This is one of the reasons some people become big losers.

3. They understand opportunity cost. They know the cost of missing out on the best opportunity. This is once again understanding the value of their scarce resources. They are not impulsive, they don't rush to take decisions, they evaluate opportunities accordingly.

Whenever winners realise they've made a mistake, they own up to it, accept it and move on without a fear of feeling embarrassed. So, they quit and move on.
Be careful of some clichés out there, don't just take things at face value, question them to understand the
context and you will clearly understand what I mean. You have the power to live your dreams!

41. Key ingredients to growth

"It's not enough to be in the right place at the right time, you must be the right person in the right place at the right time." — T. Harv Eker

Success is always looking for a good place to stay and the big question is, "are you that good place or at least developing yourself to be that good place for success to stay?" Becoming a good place for success to stay is all about being the right person in the right place at the right time and it's a lifetime commitment.

I'm reminded of Kenny Rogers' song The Gambler. One of the verses says, "You've got to know when to hold them; know when to fold them; know when to walk away; and know when to run. You never count your money when you are sitting at the table; There'll be time enough for counting when the dealing is done." And he further says, "If you gonna play the game, boy, you gonna learn to play it right." I am reminded of this song because when it comes to growth, your mindset is key.

Your mindset may be the reason you are stuck where you are and there comes a time when you have to let go of that mindset that is not serving you well — know when to fold them, know when to walk away and even run away from them. Remember that ideas without informed and persistent action will never yield results. Ideas alone may fuel frustration when you don't act on them hence the song says, "you never count your money when sitting at the table, there'll be enough time for counting when the dealing is done."

If you're going to play the game of success, you need to learn to play it right! You can choose to either have a fixed or growth/incremental mindset. If you really want to be a good place for success, you've no choice but to adopt a growth mindset. A growth mindset is based on the premise that, 'with a right strategy and enough effort, I can get better at anything.' A fixed mindset approach states that, 'you are born that way, you can't change it and you can't learn and grow.' Basically this one is based on the premise that you are stuck with what you are born with.'

Can we actually grow our cognitive abilities? About forty years ago, the answer would have been , "No, you're stuck with your brain's default wiring." Recent science shows that it's very possible and that the old thinking was wrong. The field of neuroscience has shown that, 1. You can physically grow your brain. 2. You can speed up the circuits in your brain, and 3. You can re-wire your brain for increased performance and intelligence on specific tasks. So, there you have it, you can now kiss your fixed mindset good bye!

Here are the four key ingredients to growth that you need to embrace when entering a growth mindset:

1. **Effort.** You need to know that you must put an effort in whatever you need to grow in, this is critical, important, useful and leads to growth.
2. **Challenges.** You need to accept and embrace challenges as opportunities for growth. You need to persevere and know that challenges pull you out of your comfort zone and bring out the best in you.
3. **Mistakes.** Don't hate them, don't avoid them and don't get discouraged by them, instead, use them to learn a better way.
4. **Feedback.** Don't get defensive when receiving unfavourable feedback and also more importantly, don't take it personal. Appreciate it and use it to your advantage.

When I was a teenager, one of the many games we use to play was a game of cards, we called it 'Three cards'. Three cards would be dished out to you and the chances to win would heavily depend on the order of cards you've been dealt. At times, the order of cards would be so unfavourable that some people would even cheat or disrupt the game or pull out of the game. Some would win the game though having started with a very bad combination of cards, the combination would get better every time they drew a new card from one of the decks available - closed deck or open deck. In retrospect, this is exactly what life is all about.

People with a growth mindset know that even if they've been dealt a bad hand in the game of life, they can continue to draw more cards by putting more effort and finding better strategies. This really shows that you have the power to live your dreams. Never let your past or current circumstances define your future, you can do it! Choose to enter the growth mindset and be the person that success would like to stay in.

42. Have patience

"Patience is not the ability to wait, but the ability to keep a good attitude while waiting." —Unknown

As you work to develop yourself and begin to listen to the small voice within, it's necessary that you do not panic. It's necessary that you be patient. It's necessary that you do not judge according to appearances. It's necessary that you develop stickability, that you take a stand, that you dig in.

Know that there will be some difficult times and that when you are in transition, there's going to be a drop in energy and productivity. At times, you'll know what to do, but you just won't have the energy to do it. You'll feel powerless and emotionally depleted.

It's important that you align yourself with people who are winners and are always trying to find the keys. Winners who are seeking and are going after their goals, passion and dreams with unmatched determination.

That's why it is so important that when you get up in the morning, when your feet hit the ground, you stand up and say, "Oh right life I'm ready for you!" You are fortifying yourself. You are praying and meditating and reading your goals. You know it's possible and necessary that you put your stuff to the test.

You are going out there knowing you will experience some rejections, disappointments, relationship problems and cashflow problems.

Yes, you are going out there knowing that there will some hard decisions to make and that there will be some moments when you won't know what to do. Things will be uncertain and you'll feel overwhelmed, but it's necessary that you experience that, it's a part of life.

The journey to your destiny won't be easy, it will be long and hard. All of the tough times and challenges you'll go through will lead you to become a certain kind of person. You will be toughened up in the process, you'll discover a part of you that you didn't know was there.

Even if you don't reach your goal, you can look at yourself in the mirror with respect. It's not always about winning all the time, it's about enjoying this journey called life. It's about what is it that I can learn from this? It's about what is it that life is trying to tell and teach me? What directive action do I need to take that will unlock the door to unlimited powers and possibilities that I have within myself?

As you look at what it is you want, make sure it's something you love and if you don't know what it is that you love, just toy with something until you find out that thing that has your name on it. For me, I toyed around with different things until I found that my passion was public speaking and writing and I went in all the way with excitement like a child in a candy store. I found that speaking and writing had my name on them.

So, as you look towards the future, realise that not only is it possible but necessary to test yourself.
It's necessary that your focus and pursue your dreams passionately. It's necessary that you stretch and challenge yourself every day and get yourself surrounded with people that are strange like we are, people that are dreaming like you are, people that have found something that consumes them like you are, people that have found something that excites them like you are excited.

When you do this, you will have some personal victories that you can feel good about and if there is ever a time that you must be brave, tenacious, bold and audacious, creative, relentless, resourceful and determined, that time is now.

I say to you, you are the one, you have the stuff because you have the deep hunger for something better. And you know it's there, what you have right now can't be all there is for you. I say, you are right, I affirm that for you and I recognise you for that.

You deserve the best that life has to offer, claim it!

43. It's on you

"If you want something you've never had, you must be willing to do something you've never done."
— Thomas Jefferson

When you grow up in poverty, you develop a poverty mindset. You may work hard and attain a certain level of financial success but still continue to believe that you can't afford something that you can easily afford, this is due to poverty consciousness.

You'll often hear someone saying, "I can't afford it!" This would be just to give themselves a convenient way out. This is what I mean by operating out of a poverty mindset. You deprive yourself of something you want and that you can afford simply because you are stuck in this mindset. One of the reasons you give yourself when you operate out of this mindset is that even if you were to have it, you wouldn't keep it. This mindset is difficult to break.

This is when you need someone to call you on your stuff, someone who will challenge you out of the mindset.

When good things happen to you, you pitch yourself and say, "Oh my goodness, is it really me? Am I dreaming?" In some instances, when good things are happening for you, you'll be nervous and frightened about it without any basis for it.

Now, how do you handle this stuff? Here's what we've got to do, look at the mirror and say "Hey, you can have this and you can keep this! This is not something that's passing by, that you'll have today and will be gone tomorrow! It's on you, you can make that happen and you have the power to do that."

You can change things for you. You see, it really doesn't matter what has happened to us in the past, it doesn't matter how many failures we've had, no, none of that matters. You see, you take responsibility when you acknowledge and say, "Hey, it's me! I'm the one, I've got to do this. I am the one that's going to turn this around. Yes, I've got some roadblocks, it's not easy for me but ultimately I know that these roadblocks, these obstacles, this opposition won't stop me from doing what I want to do. It can temporary cripple me or make it inconvenient but it won't stop me! It won't determine my reality."

Sadly, what many people believe is that they can't have it; that they are being unrealistic; that they are just having wild dreams — many people don't even want or ask life for anything because they don't believe they can have it.
Many of us are still where we are right now because we have not yet decided to stop being volunteer victims. We have not decided to take a stand with our lives. We have not decided that we are going to go on and begin to demonstrate a different level of consciousness in our lives.

Many of us have just surrendered, given up responsibility and spend a lot of energy being cynical, talking about why it won't work. Most people waste time building a case for their limitations and why they can't move on.

So, with all being said, I say to you, whatever it is you want, it's on you. As you look out where you want to go, it's on you to decide to move yourself there. Most of us are not doing what we want to do because we are living within the context of the conversations, opinions or the expectations that people have of us. A lot of us have been told by people we care about, people whose opinions we value, admire and believe in that we cannot do certain things and we accepted that.

Their opinions became our reality and we stopped ourselves right there in our tracks. A few of us, however, reject those things we are told we can't do, as hard as it is. So, if you don't believe in me, please, don't discourage me by telling I can't do it.

The thing is, not only do we live within the conversations and the opinions that people have of us, but a lot of us live our lives vicariously. We are not even doing what we want to do, we are doing what we feel others want us to do. Somebody once said, we are not who we think we are or what others think we are, we are who we want people to think that we are.

We go through life playing roles. When we begin to look at ourselves and search ourselves, we've got to ask ourselves, "Is this really me?

Am doing this because I want to do this? Or am I doing this because this is what is expected of me, this is something that somebody else is expecting of me?"

I remember a young lady of 15 years tried to give a speech at an event and had to be stopped and comforted by her parents because she had become too nervous on stage. After the event, I walked up to this young lady and asked her, 'Is this something you are doing because you really want to do it?' She said, "Oh no, my parents encouraged me to be a motivational speaker."

I said, "But what do you want to do? What's important to you?" She said, "I don't know, I haven't decided yet, but I'm doing this now." You see, some decisions had already been made for her, that's a lot of pressure being put on the kid, she's still learning herself.

A lot of us parents live our lives through our children. We didn't do what we wanted to do and so we are pushing our dreams through them, even though that's not in sync with what they want to do. So, as you begin to look where you want to go, it's on you, what do you want?

What gives your life a meaning right now, with the time you've left? In this moment as you look toward the future. I really like to emphasise this moment, a lot of people like to buy into the common consciousness of the illusion that we have forever, no we don't have forever. In my seminars, I like to play this song by Whitney Houston — Give me one moment in time.

It says, "Give me one moment in time when I'm more than I thought I could be. When all of my dreams are a heart-beat away and the answers are all up to me. Give me one moment in time when I'm racing with destiny, then, in that one moment of time, I will feel eternity.

You're a winner for a life time if you seize that one moment in time. Make it shine!" So, if you start living in the moment, not for the moment, you'll truly shine. Most people live their lives saying, "One day, I'm gonna!" This is because of the common consciousness that keep them from living up to their true potential. Here's something that we must begin to realise and acknowledge, we were all created to be winners, we've been endowed with greatness. I think the challenge is to begin to become in alignment with who we truly are and work diligently to manifest our greatness.

You see, through the programming of life, we get off-track. Everyone who has ever succeeded knew that it was on them, they accepted that and they took the responsibility to make it happen. Michael Korda said, "Success on any major scale requires you to accept responsibility...in the final analysis, the one quality that all successful people have...is the ability to take on responsibility."

You see most people won't take on responsibility, they won't say, "I'll make that happen. I'll deliver that!" Most people don't have that kind of guts, that kind of sense of personal power. You were born with greatness and your responsibility is to unleash it. It's on you.

44. What is my gift?

"The meaning of life is to find your gift. The purpose of life is to give it away." — Pablo Picasso

Have you ever admired the life of others and wondered what your life would be like if you had their skills, their money, or their strengths? It could be something as simple as I wish I was "that kind of mother" or "that kind of father." How about, "I wish my husband was like so and so's husband." "I wish I could own a business like them." I wish I could sing like her." "I wish I could preach like that." And the list goes on and on.

Finding your gift is similar to finding gold or diamonds. To find them, you need to follow a process.

This process is called prospecting. Prospecting is the first stage of the geological analysis of a territory. It's the physical search for minerals, fossils, precious metals or mineral specimens. This is a deliberate process which takes a long time and is hard. So, it requires tools, patience and preparedness to put in hard work over a long period of time.

What puts the light on in your eyes, that makes your eyes sparkle? Is it singing, dancing, playing a musical instrument or sport? Is it fixing something, growing something or building something? Do you have a knack for words, for language, for stories? What do people admire about you and say, "I wish I could do that"…yet it comes "naturally and easily" to you.
What do you love to do? Look forward to with eagerness and anticipation? What really brings you joy, makes you purposeful, that makes you feel you're making a positive difference?

Searching for your gift and finding it will help you serve the world, that's your purpose. This simply means your purpose is tied to your gift. The findings are always reserved for the seekers, you can't just find your gift by sitting on the couch, that's not prospecting.

Whenever I am speaking or coaching, people come to me and say, "But I don't know what my gift is, how do I find it?" This is the reason I am writing about this topic to reach out to as many people as I possibly can.

Finding your gift is like finding the raw gold or diamond, you have to patiently work so hard on it to make it valuable. You have to find people that will help you by coaching and mentoring you to refine this gift until it becomes a finished product that you are proud of and that everybody wants to have. Thomas Jefferson said, "If you want something you've never had, you must be willing to do something you've never done."

So, in closing, three things to always remember when searching for your gift:

1. Stop comparing yourself. You'll burn out in no time if you constantly measure your progress with someone else's. You are unique, special and different. You've your own path that you need to run at your own pace.

2. Be patient. You can't expect your gift to reach its full potential overnight. Forcing progress will only
produce fruit that are premature, shoddy and frankly, bitter.

3. **Be willing to invest time** and have a big room for disappointments and pain along the way, that's how it is but it's worth it.

Be willing to learn. Be a student of life. Swallow your pride and be ready to learn from everybody. Have a mentor and coach and be willing to be an apprentice. Accept that you don't know and be willing to be taught. Learning is the best thing that can get you to mastery.

I hope this helps you clarify some doubts and get started on this journey of finding your gift/s and work on them until they shine!

The world has long been waiting for your shine, now it's the time, shine!

45. What makes you come alive?

"Most of us go through life as complete strangers to our highest selves." — Veli Ndaba — 'The Engineered Mind — to WIN'

Let me tell you the strange story of Willie Sutton, a prolific American bank robber. After many years of robbing banks, he was caught a few times and jailed. He escaped three times from different prisons.

Later on in his "career", he was asked why he was robbing banks and he responded, "That's where the money is."
He said, "I loved robbing banks. I was more alive when I was inside a bank robbing it than any other time in my life. I enjoyed everything about it so much that one or two weeks later, I'd be out looking for the next job. But to me, the money was the chips, that's all. I really wasn't doing it for money!" He said. He didn't use a real gun (or if real, it was unloaded) and relied mostly on his disguises to succeed in his robberies. This earned him two nicknames, "Willie the Actor" and "Slick Willie" His answer "That's where the money is" to the question why he robbed banks, evolved into a corollary, the Willie Sutton Rule.

This rule is used in management accounting; it stipulates that activity-based accounting should be applied where the highest costs occur, because that's where the biggest savings can be found. It is also often invoked to medical students as a metaphor for focusing on the most likely diagnosis, rather than wasting time and money investigating every conceivable possibility.

How incredible is it that we can learn from a bank robber? But let's take it one step further: like Willie, what makes you come alive when you do it? That thing that makes money to be like chips to you? That thing that you always look forward to? For me, it's speaking, writing and coaching to make a difference in people's lives.

You have the power to live your dreams, it's not somewhere out there, it's within you, you were born with it, unleash it!

46. Don't comfort your problem, confront it

"Problems are like washing machines. They twist, they spin and knock us around. But in the end we come out cleaner, brighter and better than before." — Unknown

What is the secret ingredient of tough people that enables them to succeed? Why do they survive the tough and challenging times when others are overcome by them? Why do they win when others lose? Why do they soar when others sink?

Well, studies conducted on these people have all shown that it's how they perceive their problems. They understand some principles that pertain to all problems. These people do not allow their problems to push them around but instead, they allow their dreams to lead them. You may be labouring under the illusion that you've a problem, when in fact you lack the courage to make a tough and right decision. Your life may be miserable right now because of some people who make it so.

You may be stressing and trying different ideas on how to change these people so they can understand you better when in fact you don't need that. In this instance, all you need is courage to let them go! This requires self-confidence. So, confidence is one quality these people have and it is learnable.

Let me share with you the principles I alluded to earlier about how tough people see their problems:

1.   Every living human being has problems.

This is principle number 1 on which they operate: they don't take problems personally. They don't feel like they are being attacked. If you are unemployed for an example, you think the job would

solve all your problems. Countless people have jobs they don't like. They are giving five days a week to unhappiness. They work to live rather than live to work. They focus on the unenjoyable aspects of their jobs. They drag their feet getting to the workplace. Some people think their problems stem from the fact that they have to report to a boss. They falsely assume that they would be happy if they could be self-employed. It's true that they might find some enjoyment in such a working arrangement, but many self-employed people have more problems than those who work for others. Retired people also have problems. Many are bored, some become depressed soon after retiring because they no longer feel productive or useful. Many actually wish they could be back at work. So, every living human being has problems, don't take yours personally.

2. Every problem has a limited life span.
History teaches us that every problem has a life span. No problem is permanent. The problem you have right now will pass. Your problem will not live forever, you are tougher than your problems.

Storms always give way to the sun. Winter always gives way to the springtime. Your storm will pass, just don't comfort it, confront it!

3. Every problem will change you.
Tough people know that problems are not meant to leave us the same way they found us. They embrace the fact that problems are like washing machines. They twist you, spin you, knock you around and even mercilessly drag you around kicking and screaming but by the time they are done with you, you're stronger and better than before. Don't approach your problems with a victim's mindset, embrace them because they carry with them a seed of greatness.

4. You can choose what your problem will do to you.
Whatever you do, never let a problem become an excuse for your inaction. Whenever you are dealing with a problem, don't think emotionally. Don't let your emotions decide for you, use your brain. Larry De Angelo said it succinctly, "Life is like a grinding stone — it can polish you or pulverise you — depending on how you position yourself."

Remember to calm yourself down in front of a problem, don't think emotionally. Train yourself to control your emotional brain and engage your thinking brain more because it always finds the answers when given a chance to look for them, trust it.

Once again, your problem is not the worst problem in the world and you're not the only one who has it. That problem is there for a season. It is there to change you and grow you for the next season,
embrace it instead of taking it personally. Choose to be polished by your problem rather than to be crushed and ground into powder by it, you have the power to make that choice.

There was swine flu soon after World War 1, smallpox followed, HIV came and is still there, now it's COVID-19. What does this all tell us? This too shall pass, just do what you need to do — take precautionary measures and be responsible and that will ensure we emerge victorious.

47. It's time to reinvent yourself

"It's not the size of the dog in the fight, it's the size of the fight in the dog." — Mark Twain

Fierceness is not necessarily a matter of physical size, but rather a mental or psychological attitude. Don't try to change the world, change yourself. Why? Because the whole world is only relative to the eyes that are looking at it.

Re-inventing or changing yourself requires that you take some risks, starting with the small ones of course. Dr David Viscott, author of the book Risking said, "If you cannot risk, you cannot grow; if you cannot grow, you cannot be your best; if you cannot be your best, you cannot be happy; if you cannot be happy than, what else is there?"

So, for you to be the person you've never been, you have to be the person you've never been and that demands you to take some risks. You see, in the end the people who fail are those that don't even try. The only thing that stands between a person and what s/he wants from life is often merely the will to try it and the faith to believe that it is possible.

When I was in high school, my teachers advised me that since I was good in mathematics and science, engineering was going to be perfect for me. There was a shortage of engineers and the financial reward was amazing.
Then, I studied mechanical engineering and I worked as an engineer. At the beginning, I must admit, the focus was on financial reward. I climbed the corporate ladder and got into management levels. The mon- ey, the status of the position was good. But the void between me and what I was doing started growing. The feeling of being a stranger in the field I was academically qualified to be in, grew stronger and stronger by the day. I started looking forward to knock off times, Fridays and hated my Sunday evenings because they literally transported me to my workplace. I got to a point where something had to give and surely it did. Today I'm a professional speaker (motivational/business and leadership), life/business coach and an author of four books. This is what I was born to do.

Every day of my life I see and speak to people who are unhappy and stuck in wrong careers (with aca- demic qualifications), just like I was, but are lacking courage to confront themselves. Being in a job or environment that doesn't suit you, steals your creativity, joy, peace and harmony within you.

You become a negative energy in the workplace and wherever you go. Being and feeling stuck in life is an awful place to be. When you feel stuck, it feels as though you are literally just spinning your wheels in the mud and are running around in circles. It also feels as though no matter what you do or say, nothing will ever change for the better and you'll be stuck in a rut forever.

If you're not careful, being stuck in life can magnify the fear, guilt, shame and/or apathy you're already feeling.

You can become even more stuck than you already are. So, rather than doing nothing and allow- ing yourself to get sucked into a really terrible rabbit hole, let me share few ways to reinvent yourself so you — and your life — can start to become unstuck:

1. Clear emotional clutter: It's easier to deal with physical clutter because you can see it. Emotional clutter is much more difficult because it's affecting how you think and do everything. Yet often, you're not even aware of it all. The way you start to conquer emotional clutter is by becoming aware of your actions and then becoming aware of how you're feeling throughout the day. This means asking your- self questions like: 1. How am I feeling? 2. Why do I feel this way? Is there anything I can change for the better in this moment?

3. **Invest in a life coach:** You cannot resolve your issues with the same energy you created them with. Be open to new ideas and new ways of doing things. This you can achieve by getting a life coach that will help you see you are blinded to.

A coach a will help you challenge yourself to get yourself un- stuck but be patient with yourself, it takes a bit of time

3. Take it slow

When we get stuck, we want to become unstuck as quickly as possible. What we don't realise is that sometimes, we get stuck for a reason. When we take the time to look at ourselves and how we feel about what's currently going on, it gives us the ability to make small changes that can often have a huge, lasting results.

You also don't need to make huge, dramatic changes in order to reinvent your- self. Often making small, slow changes are the best way to become a new, better version of yourself that is easy for you to maintain. This means you've taken the time to really become a better version of yourself — rather than simply acting it out.

You have the power to live your dreams, unleash it!

48. What will your message be?

"Tell them I tried to feed the hungry. Tell them I tried to clothe the naked. Tell them I tried to help somebody."
— Martin Luther King, Jr

This was the message Martin Luther King junior left behind for future generations. What will your message be? If you were to record your parting message today, would you with conviction say that you tried to feed the hungry? Would you say you tried to clothe the naked and that you really, I mean really, tried to help somebody? What evidence would be used to back up your claim?

If you have a challenge in answering these questions, then, you better hurry up and do something before your time runs out of time! It's time to commit to your commitments and keep the main thing, the main thing.

I recently wrote about commitment where I said that commitment is doing what you said you'll do, when you said you'll do it whether you like it not.

It's not about doing things because you feel like doing them. Courage and willpower are developed when you do what needs to be done, whether you like it or not. To commit is about getting off the fence by taking a firm and bold decision, compromising and improvising.

These four are siblings and can never be separated, especially if one wants to live a meaningful life:

1. Taking a firm and bold decision.
2. Sacrificing certain things.
3. Improvising — doing what you can, using what you have, wherever you are. It's that level of maturity of not
complaining and mourning about what you don't have, and instead maximising what you have.
4. Committing to your decision.

For you to see beyond the storm, you need to be a possibility thinker. Possibility thinking is the management of ideas. There's time management, money management, self-management and people management, energy management, etc. Possibility thinking focuses on the management of ideas and thoughts. So, management is the control of a resource in order to minimise waste and maximise the development of latent possibilities.

In 2005, the National Science Foundation published an interesting article summarising research on human thoughts per day. It was found that the average person has about 12 000 to 60 000 thoughts per day. Of those thousands of thoughts, 80% were negative and 95% were exactly the same repetitive thoughts as the day before.

This clearly shows that one of the tendencies of the mind is to focus on the negative and 'play the same songs' over and over again. There was another interesting study (Leahy, 2005, Study of Cornell University), that concluded that 97% of our worries are baseless and result from an unfounded pessimistic perception.

Unfortunately, these baseless worries are a major source of stress, tension and cause exhaustion not only for the mind, but also for the physical body. I am sharing this information so that you'll be aware of your thoughts and manage them better.

So, as we can see from the above, a vast majority of the ideas and thoughts are negative. Possibility thinking is the disciplined separation of positive thoughts from negative ones.
Positive thoughts are those that hold undeveloped potential for good. Possibility thinkers always search and sieve the good ideas from the bad ones. Impossibility thinkers, on the other hand, are people who instinctively react negatively to ideas that have potential for good. Impossibility thinkers impulsively look for reasons why it can't be done.

Life keeps on teaching us that storms are in many ways good for us. They draw something out of us that calm seas don't. Steve Rizzo said it succinctly, "Don't wait for the storms of your life to pass. Learn to dance in the rain." The mind will always play tricks on you, be awake and watch out, you are in charge.

Like any movie that you might have watched, the heroes go through a lot of adversity and one wonders why they have to endure such challenges and why do they have to put themselves through so much suffering? Well, this is because beyond that pain, they see something wonderful, not only for themselves but for others as well.

You were born to make a difference. You were born for greatness. Your heart knows the truth, listen to it. Nelson Mandela said, "There is no passion to be found playing small — in settling for a life that is less than the one you are capable of living." This, I fully agree with, hence you are reading this. What message will you leave for the future generations?

You have the power to make your life count, Rise and Shine!

49. Confidence, oh!
What a skill to have!

"When you have a lot of confidence and you feel like nobody can beat you, it's game over for everyone else."
— Jason Day

The dictionary defines confidence as "the feeling or belief that one can rely on someone or something; firm trust." When we feel confident in ourselves, we know and trust in our ability to do what we have promised. Same applies when we have confidence in others, we know and trust in their ability to do

what they have promised. This means that as is our confidence, so is our capacity.

I have two boys, Ntokozo and Sanele, 20 and 17 years old, respectively. I keep planting these thoughts in their minds, to win themselves over and to never be made to feel they are nobodies or less than

somebody else. I want them to grow up knowing that, no matter what, their lives matter, they count and they deserve to be alive and to connect with the highest that's within them.

You see, many of us struggle with confidence issues. In an age of social media, it can be difficult not to compare ourselves with other people and end up losing sight of what's important.

We might lack confidence at work, in public speaking, or in meeting new people, which makes us fear that we aren't taken seriously or that we won't meet new friends or a significant other. Confidence is a beautiful thing to possess.

Looking back over my life, I talked myself so many times out of things because I lacked confidence. I held back a number of times from saying what I wanted to say because more confident people were speaking up. If you were the one of the quiet ones at school then you will know what I mean. The loudest are the ones that are heard, and this continues throughout your adult life. Then I came to the realisation that if I was going to do any of the things I wanted to do in life, I needed to find confidence, lots of it.

Many people are stuck in situations, careers, jobs and relationships that are not doing them any good, that are toxic to them. Why don't they get out? I hear you ask, well, the main reason for all of this is the lack of self-confidence. They don't see themselves outside of these toxic situations that daily drain their energy and kill their brilliant ideas, it's truly a sad situation. Great ideas keep dropping into their minds without being taken seriously, they are never executed until they sort of rot in there. So, the mind becomes the graveyard of brilliant ideas.

Our tendency is not to do anything about the incredible ideas that come to our minds. Years later, when we read that somebody else has turned an idea into a great success, we may lament to ourselves, *'I thought about that once, why didn't I do something about it?'*

The thought of picking a new career in mid-life is probably an impossibility in your imagination. Part of this insecurity or lack of self-confidence is because we tend to develop a negative self-image based on our low position on the ladder of life.

People think that if they were really brilliant, they would be president of some corporation.
I write and speak a lot about greatness. Greatness doesn't depend upon your position in life, but upon your respect of the positive ideas that flow into your imagination.

After reading self-improvement books and articles, I slowly began to realise what real confidence is and
how I could have it too. This is what I discovered:

1. **Confidence is not a personality trait:** Think of how differently you act in front of your family and friends than in front of strangers or in a room full of people. How confident you are completely
changes depending on the situation and context. It's not set and how you react to those situations can be adapted and developed over time.

2. **Confidence takes practice:** I use to be shy speaking in front of strangers and in a room full of people. I started attending Toastmasters International, an organisation that helps people confront their fears and develop public speaking skills. Right now, that's none of my worries. I speak in front of thousands of people now with so much ease. So, it's all about practise, practise and practise.

3. **You don't have to be loud to be confident:** Ever heard the phrase 'Those who shout the loudest often have nothing to say'? You don't have to force your point on others to be heard. You have to believe in yourself though. Confidence is contagious, so is lack of it.

When others are busy putting their money on expensive outfits and other material things, invest yours on developing self-confidence because the most beautiful thing you can ever wear is confidence.

50. How to win yourself from mediocrity

"All compromise is based on give and take, but there can be no give and take on fundamentals. Any compromise on mere fundamentals is a surrender. For it is all give and no take." — Mahatma Gandhi

These are the words of wisdom which must be understood for what they are. To me, they mean that a person or even an organisation starts to fall apart when they compromise their beliefs. Over time, these compromises can undermine, or even eliminate, the core value of the person.

Until this fact dawns on you, you'll be stuck in mediocrity. Whenever I speak on different stages and in my coaching sessions, I get to see people who are hungry for a new and better life but can't see beyond their current circumstances; they think and believe what they see is all there is in their lives. My purpose is to help people revive hope, self-belief and gain confidence in themselves to see beyond their current chal- lenges.

The first thing to do is to confess that you are stuck. On confession, Gandhi said, "Confession of errors is like a broom which sweeps away the dirt and leaves the surface brighter and clearer. I feel stronger for confes- sion." When you confess your errors in judgement, your mind and your soul gets brighter and clearer for you to adopt a new and different perspective on life.

Winning yourself from mediocrity in order for you to claim your greatness starts with an understanding of what mediocrity is. Mediocrity is a world you live in that is bound on the North by Compromise; on the South by Indecision; on the East by Past Thinking and finally on the West by Lack of Vision. It's critical to understand that your world has been kept intact by these four anchors.

For you, to move or shake them, you need to unpack them:

1. Northern side — Compromise. The dictionary defines compromise as the expedient/convenient accep- tance of standards that are lower than is desirable. Here my focus is fundamentals. You can compromise on other things but your fundamentals. Do you know what your fundamentals are? That's a starting point! Some key fundamentals you shouldn't compromise on:

- Self-respect and self-discipline. Never give up on these because they are your powers for life.
- Dignity. Never let anyone take away your pride and dignity. Always know that you matter and that your life has an ultimate purpose and significance.

- Your individuality. Never compromise on your qualities and values just for people to like you. Life is to express yourself not impress others. So, be yourself! Your character defines you, don't lose your identity.
- Health. Never compromise on your health, take good care of it. Your health is your wealth.
- Your dreams and aspirations. Flatly refuse to be a killer and a graveyard of your dreams.
- Family. They are your foundation, pillars and everything. Don't compromise on them for anyone or anything.

Just on a lighter note: someone once said, "A friend is a God's way of apologising to us for our families." So, God knew that he'll give you some siblings and those cousins that are letting you down almost every time without fail but are stuck with them, hahahaha! So, when you choose friends, choose them well!

2. Southern side — Indecision. One of my favourite quotes when I speak on this topic is, "The road of life is paved with squirrels who couldn't make a decision," unknown author. In life you have to take a decision and stick with it, if it proves to be wrong, pivot without losing balance and take another one. That's why there are training courses offered on decision making, empower yourself by investing in them. Stop procrastinat- ing and do something.

3. Eastern side — Past thinking. There are people who are stuck in the past. Whenever they open their mouths, it's about the past failures, disappointments, successes, etc. It's all about the past. Yes, we are products of our past but we should never be the prisoners of it. Whenever I look at the past, I see many things that I failed at not because I was a bad person, but because I didn't know better. It would therefore be very harsh and unfair of me to define myself by my past. Sometimes when I want to have a good laugh, I just reflect on my past and boy oh boy! I crack up on seeing how naïve I was, that's me!

4. Western side — Lack of vision. My favourite quote I mostly use whenever I talk on this subject is by Helen Keller. She said, "The only thing worse than being blind is to have sight but no vision." She was 87 years old when she died and had lost her sight at the age of 19 months. This means she had been blind for 85 years and 5 months, yet she said these words. So, disability is not the lack of physical eyes, but lack of vision. This means disability is not more about physical limbs but inability to connect with the unseen, the future. This is very profound. Are you connected with your future?

Winning yourself over from mediocrity, requires you to correct the errors in judgement regarding the fundamentals you've compromised on, decisiveness, not being imprisoned by your past and having a clear vision of the future. Finally, remember, any compromise on mere fundamentals is a surrender, for it is all give and no take.

You have the power to live your dreams, claim them!

51. In search of self

"The worst thing in life is waking up old and realizing you became so good at the wrong thing." — Joel Salatin

One of my coaching sessions recently got me very emotional. I had this 60 year who has a doctorate (Ph.D.) in his field, has been working for an organisation for 35 years and is going on retirement soon. When I asked him about his plans for retirement, he mumbled and eventually said that was the reason he had come to see me. He was scared of facing the uncertain future outside of the organisation he has dedicated his entire adult life serving. Uncertainty was written all over his face.

We are all busy doing something, we invest our precious time and energy in it. How often do you pause and honestly ask yourself why you're doing it? Are you doing it because you are in a habit of doing it? Are you doing it because you've been told to do it? Are you doing it just because most people are doing it? This is like wearing something that you don't necessarily like but wear it because it's in fashion or it's the 'in-thing'.

You see, it is crucial to think about these things because it shows that you're aware of your actions, that you are watching yourself in action, which is truly critical. One of the saddest things in life is having a goal and achieving it but later realise that you didn't really need or wish to pursue it at all. Don't just get lost in a life of existence, of the here and now, search for the life of purpose.

The Temptations (American vocal group) has a song called — I've Never Been to Me. In this song, there's where it says: "Ooh I've been to Georgia and California, oh, anywhere I could run…. Oh I've been to Nice and the Isle of Greece.

I've sipped champagne on a yacht. I moved like Harlow in Monte Carlo and showed them what I've got. I've been to paradise, but I've never been to me. Hey, you know what paradise is? It's a lie, a fantasy we create about people and places as we'd like them to be."

The "paradise" that is meant in the song is the supposed glamorous and dissipated lifestyle many ordinary people aspire to, i.e. hanging out with important people, travelling to exotic places, showing off what you've got, etc. This song in the main is about regret of the lost time chasing unnecessary things and wishing someone had spoken sense into you. This is an example of waking up old one day and realising that you mastered the art of doing the wrong things, you became so good at wasting your life. You and I have to learn from this and avoid it.

Most people who are employed are so focused on the here and now, they see retirement as something very far away and some even think that retirement is "paradise". Yes, they are under the false illusion that real life will start after retirement. In my life coaching experience, very few people have plans for beyond retirement, they are hoping that things will just happen. Well, let me tell you this, things don't just happen, they happen just. The purpose of life is not just to have a job and pay the bills but it's to express our gifts because that's what connects us with our true selves.

If you were to be retired today, I'm saying 'retired' because most people don't retire by choice or because they want to but 'are retired' by the organisations they work for. So, again, if you were to be retired today, what would you do with your life for the next, say 20 to 30 years? What would you do that would fulfil you and make you look forward to every day? How would you contribute to the world?

You see, this is why you need to know yourself. What are your strengths? What are your natural inclinations? What turns you on? What injects you with energy? No one will teach you these, they need you to engage with them your- self. You don't want to wait until you retire to work on these, the sooner you start the better.

Think of these three responsibilities:

1. Responsibility to self: You were not born just to make a living, but to live your making and it's your making that should help you make a living. Be the best of whatever you are.

2. Responsibility to employer/client: This is to do the best you can to improve the quality of life for your organisation or client that pays you for your services. Don't just do what's enough to get by, give it your all and add value.

3. Responsibility to humanity: A life well lived is the one of knowing that someone else's life is much better today because you lived. Greed is going to the grave with your unused gift, having never shared your gift with humanity because you only focused on the job just to pay the bills and missed out on true living. The world has long been waiting for your gifts, take them out and share them! Today.

52. Different types of acceptance

Many psychologists believe that one of the reasons why most people only utilize up to 14% of their potential is that they are never happy with themselves and they have a low level of self-acceptance.

Two types of acceptance exist:
1. **Passive acceptance**. This means that we need to accept the things we can't change, like weather, hours in a day and number of days in a year, your place of birth, family background, etc.
2. **Active acceptance**. This refers to the fact that we shouldn't permanently accept the things we can change as those we can't, like being overweight, employer, a career, a romantic partner, etc.

Some people mistaken passive acceptance with learned helplessness. These two are not the same. Learned helplessness is the giving up reaction, the quitting response that stems from a belief that nothing you do matters. This is mostly caused by negative conditioning such as criticism received from parents, teachers, and the community as a child. Through my coaching sessions, I help people raise their level of self-awareness around this and change the situation. Let me help you live your dreams!

Make failure your teacher, not your undertaker! No, don't let failure bury you, let it inspire you to rise up and claim your stuff.

53. Conclusion

"Whatever you do, work at it with all your heart, as working for the Lord, not for human masters." — Colossians 3:23

This brings me to the end of this book and as I write this conclusion, the whole world is battling with the Covid-19 pandemic. Every human being faces great health, social and economic challenges. You no doubt also have some challenges you are dealing with at present.

I hope that reading my book has filled you with hope and enthusiasm for the future. I hope that the book inspires you to greater heights no matter who you are, where you are, where you come from or how Covid-19 impacts humanity. Never stop dreaming and achieving. Go for it!

I urge you to reach greater heights, to reach personal greatness, because you are made in the image and likeness of God our Creator (Genesis 1:27). Not because you are better than someone else or de- serve better than someone else.

Please never harm or hurt anyone on your way to greater heights. In fact, help others to climb with you as they're also made in the image and likeness of God!

Please remember that self-awareness is not the same as self-obsession. Be kind to others and never forget that we are part of a bigger picture, "Umuntu ngumuntu ngabantu", the principle of Ubuntub that "I am, because you are".

Some of the best gifts you can ever give are the following:
- to your enemy, forgiveness
- to an opponent, tolerance
- to a friend, your heart
- to a customer, service
- to all, charity
- to every child, a good example
- to yourself, respect
- to a reader, an end to your book

I wish you much success, good health and happiness today and always. Thank you for your time, thank you for reading my book.

Endorsement

This is where Veli's readers have their say... you're also invited to give your feedback by emailing him directly at veli@velindaba.com.

From: **Enock Mdlalose**
Longtime friend

"Mr Ndaba, I'm happy to see you doing what you loved from your early age. I remember when I first met you in standard 7 in 1987 (now known as grade 9) and what made me notice the talent in you, was the debate on "corporal punishment distorts the way that life is sacred" at school. We were on the same team and we enjoyed crushing our opponent's points and there you excelled. I wanted to know more about you, I visited you at your home and listened to the type of music you played, which was different and somehow boring to what I was used to. I later realised that it was a cool and informative music from Radio Metro which was difficult to tune into that time, you had to tune into the Medium Wave Frequency (MW) not the frequency modulation on stereo these days. You motivated me to tune in and listen to Metro FM as well and I liked the way you expressed yourself mimicking radio presenters like Lawrence Dube, Wilson B Nkosi and Grant Shakoane (your personal favourite) and many others, especially from Friday evenings, Top 40 on Saturday and weekend rendezvous by Grant Shakoane on Sunday afternoons.

Besides debates and your beautiful music, you knew how to balance schoolwork and house work, collect water since water taps were few kilometres away, and also play soccer.

After high school we lost contact with each other for about 4 years. When we met again, you were a qualified engineer. And when we started catching up on news, you told me about a decision tree – in my mind I thought of a place where you sit under the tree and make decisions, hahahaha! You elaborated the meaning and I was impressed, and I saw the light. I realised that you were still on track to achieve your dreams and here you are today still watering our roots. Keep up the good work, you were born for this, keep winning. Keep shining. I wish you what's best for you and your family. Cheers."

From: **Verona Duwarkar**
Business and Life Coach, Author, CEO
"I met Veli at the beginning of his journey in the personal development space and from that moment I knew that I had found someone that understood his Life Purpose. His ability to inspire, motivate, teach, and share wisdom in a way that is easily understood by his audience makes him easy to relate to and to learn from.

He ensures that you have fun and have some good laughs while learning. He is one of the most driven individuals I know and is constantly experimenting with new ways of improving his clients' lives.

Over the years I have watched him excel in his writing — three books and growing...I remember a time when we were both still talking about writing, what we would write about etc...and here he is, writing articles for various platforms, speaking to large audiences, living his best life! His writing is honest, and anyone can relate and implement key learnings from his books and articles — this can and will bring positive change to your life.

Veli is a humble and grounded person who takes his profession very seriously and has a passion for growth, education and the greater good of humanity. He is an inspiration to me — I learn from him all the time. I am fortunate and blessed to call him my Awesome Friend!"

From: **Salamina (Sally) Mokome Inspired reader and follower**

"Life is difficult, we all say that, but I say it is full of challenges and it is with these challenges that we become better people. It is during such times where the best comes out of us, when we are out of the comfort zone. One day, while I was listening to the radio, I heard Veli Ndaba talk about his book You Are Born To Win and how fear from the past can stop you from achieving what is your calling and why you were born in the first place. It was like he was talking to me because I knew I could do better with my life.

Afterwards I saw his articles in our local newspaper, what a sound mind! When I contacted him on Facebook, he started sending me regular motivational pieces. I was starting to be tired of being tired, of complaining. I went on to attend one of his seminars and guess what, I couldn't eat and sleep, I had to start working on my subconscious mind. You Are Born to Win is his first book; his second book is Your Dream Is Calling You. His weekly articles and posts are 'vitamins' that keep me inspired and focused on my goals. I would like to say thank you Veli Ndaba for sharing your gift with us and may God abundantly bless you. Visit his Facebook page and see for yourself. Make A Change."

From: **Ikageng Mophulane Inspired reader and follower**

"I feel honoured to own all of your books, Mr Veli Ndaba, they were instrumental for me in finding my purpose and believing in myself. I realised that I can apply the knowledge I got from your books and weekly articles in all dimensions of my life. Your continuous inspiration motivates me. Just last year I enrolled with York Academy and I got a leadership skills certificate. Thank you so much, my leader. God bless you and your team."

From: **Jameson "JK" Mogafe Director at B3 Insurance Brokers**

"People come and people go, but very few get to be impactful enough to be remembered. I had the honour and privilege to meet Mr Veli Ndaba sometime in 2019 when I attended one of his in-house seminars.

He gets you going without sensationalising and whipping up emotions, which I find most motivational speakers doing. He presents with ease and calmness that ensures that whatever he says, sinks in. When my company planned a strategic session, I remembered Veli and we enlisted his services. He did very well, and we remain grateful for his input. He is one amongst the few people I know who do not read to forget."

From: **Phineas Manamela**
Operations Executive- Masscash Retail (Division of Massmart-Walmart)

"Veli Ndaba's book, Set Your Soul On Fire" is a brilliant collection of articles which I have become accustomed to every Sunday (I call them my "Sunday dose of wisdom" in preparation for the week ahead). I can attest that I have at times felt completely challenged and at others I have had to think deeply about my approach to life.

Veli's articles helped me to reflect and make a shift... One such article is titled "Are you just Being Book Smart?". Before I read this article, I was caught in a race to see how many books I could read in a month, which titles are a "must-read".

It was a race to nowhere. Since reading the article, I have pulled out of the rat-race and focused my energy on implementing what I read with specific focus on perfecting my own art and complementing my own skills.
In the article, Veli writes "Education is not memorising known facts, moulding you and turning you into a robot (which unfortunately is the case) but it should inspire and support your natural longing to know." These are incredible words of wisdom that challenge us to think differently about why we acquire information, and most importantly how we use it to fulfil our own potential.
This is a real must read! Thank you Veli."

From: **Dr Musa Mayayise Cardiologist**

"Success is usually seen in its outward manifestations, i.e. the expensive cars, houses and other
sought-after material. However, the real magic of success is the transformation that happens on the inside, in your soul when you doubt yourself and refuse to give up, when the journey becomes too painful to continue but you continue anyway, when you fall down and decide to get up and give it another shot one more time.
The question is what to do when doubt, fatigue and all other enemies of success strike you along the way. That is where Set Your Soul on Fire! gives you a recharge. What if you are unable to get started because of fear or other limitations?

Set Your soul On Fire is the fuel you need to give yourself that push-start. When I read the manuscript, I thought I would eat it up in one sitting but some of the chapters hit me very hard. I had to put down the book (manuscript) from time to time and do some thinking and evaluation of myself and that is the impact of Veli Ndaba's writing."

8.

From: **Johannes Lehutso**
Senior Pastor of Good Shepherd Ministries, Chairperson and Lecturer at World Outreach Bible College and Training Specialist in Life Assurance

Hi Mzi (Cuz)
I am thrilled with the opportunity to pre-read your book. Your introduction has "awakened the giant within me" in the words of Anthony Robbins. You used great and power phrases that are life changing. The introduction is a thrill for me. I love it. The Power of Purpose has shifted my paradigm to begin prioritising before inviting partners to join me. This chapter is practical and well thought through. The Best Gifts You Can Ever Give! The six steps are user friendly and when people apply them in their lives, the out- come will be great results. Understanding the Law of Harvest is helping me to re-look at great seeds I have within me.
I am busy re-evaluating the successes I had in the past and how I can continue to maximise on the knowledge I have. I am privileged to be reading your book and do know that my soul is set on fire and there is no going back.

If people apply what you are giving, they will never settle for less in their lives. I love the way you conclude each sub-title for instance you say; "Let's do it! Let's join hands in making this beautiful world of ours a much better place than we found it!" These words make me feel you have joined forces with me and I have a partner in my development journey. The reader is not going it
alone because you, "The Coach" are there with him/her each step of the way. I love it.

Fail Fast & It's All in Your Attitude. Wow! I know many people who have been immobilized because of Fear of Failing. This chapter takes away the myth which destabilizes people from venturing into doing what they want. Old beliefs have been dismantled and freedom is reigning in my spirit. Statements like: "Some people are born great, others achieve greatness and some have greatness thrusted upon them" need to be questioned. We are All born to win. We are all born to be great. All we need is to fix our attitudes toward life. Yes! My soul is on fire. This book truly sets one's soul on fire with practical steps that are easy to apply. The one ingredient every one of us need is the habit of practising over and over until it becomes second nature. The analogy of A River and A Dam drives the message home. I have chosen to be a river! I am enthused by the power phrases that are packed under each sub-title in the book. Each page has life-changing and thought provoking statements that are practical. Every person who wants to succeed
and exploit greatness that is within, needs to action the lessons that are packaged in this inspiring book.

Thank you Mzi for the opportunity for me to do introspection. I am privileged to be reading your books. I do know that "people fail not because they do not know what to do, but because they do not do what they know" Author unknown.

May great success come your way Mzi.

Sekusile TS

Featuring Veli Ndaba – 'The Engineered Mind – to WIN'

Service Offerings Under One Roof:

Motivational Speaking:
The challenges of life can bring you down to your knees and make you forget your greatness. Let me, Veli Ndaba, with my motivational talks ignite the fire within you so you can re-connect with your greatness!

Coaching | Consulting | Training
The power to change your future is in your hands, use it! Partner with me, Veli Ndaba - 'The Engineered Mind - to Win' on the journey to help you reinvent yourself.

Books
Great minds, dead or alive, have shared their secrets of success in books. Reading books helps you tap into their minds and get you ahead of the pack. Grab your copy today!

Seminars | Workshops
Get inspired seminars and workshops provide you the platform to increase your self-awareness and network with like-minded people. Join in today!

Venue Hire: Boardrooms & Conference Room
We learn, think and become more creative in a peaceful environment. Sekusile Premium Venues provide you with tranquility and help you connect with the highest that is in you!

Call us today and let's help you structure your desired package from the above listed service offerings.

Contact details:
Tel: (010) 591 1197
admin@sekusile-ts.co.za • www.sekusile-ts.co.za
16 Newquay Road, New Redruth, Alberton • -26.269642, 28.123916